# WHITHER LATIN AMERICA?

*Carlos Fuentes*
*Paul Johnson*
*Leo Huberman*
*Andrew Gunder Frank*
*Paul M. Sweezy*

# WHITHER LATIN AMERICA?

*Harvey O'Connor*
*Francisco Juliao*
*Sebastian Salazar Bondy*
*Manuel Augustin Aguirre*

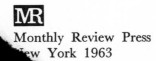
Monthly Review Press
New York 1963

# Foreword

In the last few years North America has become conscious of Latin America. Pick up a copy of almost any newspaper or mass-circulation magazine and examine its contents: the chances are that it will contain material on one or more of the Latin American countries, or perhaps on the region as a whole. And yet, despite this spate of printed matter, North Americans are profoundly ignorant of the realities of Latin America. They know next to nothing about its history; the image they have of its present is distorted to the point of falsehood; and the vision they have of its future is unrelated to the tendencies and forces that are shaping the destinies of our neighbors to the south.

The reasons for this ignorance are not far to seek. Speaking in historical terms, Latin America is in the throes of one of the great revolutionary upheavals of modern times. It began in Mexico in 1910; its latest manifestation is in Cuba. Long before another half century has passed, it will have shaken and transformed the whole vast region. But those who dominate the United States today do not like revolutions. They have adopted the posture of a modern King Canute commanding the revolutionary waves to subside. The American people, who have been nurtured on their own revolutionary tradition, must be persuaded to accept and support this posture. They must therefore be lied to, and that is the role which the mass-communication media have taken it upon themselves to perform. It is that simple.

In this little volume we have brought together a dozen ticles which appeared in MONTHLY REVIEW, most of them or 1963, and all but one in the 1960's. (Harvey "Venezuela: A Study in Imperialism" appeared ept for details, could as well have appeared not pretend that they tell the whole truth hey have no such ambitious aim. But many truths and that the overall is accurate and reliable. They

1

answer the question posed by the title, and they do so un-ambiguously: Latin America is headed for a profound revolu-tionary transformation.

There is nothing here on Cuba. The reason is that Monthly Review Press has published four books on Cuba in the last three years, and the magazine has carried many articles on the Cuban Revolution. This volume is intended to complement these earlier works, not to add to them.

Paul M. Sweezy
Leo Huberman

April 10, 1963

# Contents

# THE ARGUMENT OF LATIN AMERICA: WORDS FOR THE NORTH AMERICANS

## BY CARLOS FUENTES

Last spring, one of the big TV networks arranged a debate between Carlos Fuentes, the well-known young Mexican novelist, and Richard Goodwin, Assistant Secretary of State for Latin American affairs. The U.S. Embassy in Mexico, however, refused a visa to Señor Fuentes and the debate never took place. An effort was then made to place Señor Fuentes' prepared text before the American public via one of the mass-circulation magazines. None was interested. After you have read the text below, you will understand why both the State Department and the mass media are so anxious to keep the views of a leading Latin American intellectual from the American public. As the son of a Mexican diplomat, Carlos Fuentes went to school in Washington, D.C., and is as much at home in the English as in the Spanish language.—The Editors

South of your border, my North American friends, lies a continent in revolutionary ferment—a continent that possesses immense wealth and nevertheless lives in a misery and a desolation you have never known and barely imagine. Two hundred million persons live in Latin America. One hundred and forty million of them work virtually as serfs. Seventy million are outside the monetary economy. One hundred million are illiterate. One hundred million suffer from endemic diseases. One hundred and forty million are poorly fed.

Today, these miserable masses have decided to put an end to this situation. Latin America, for centuries nothing more than an object of historical exploitation, has decided to change —into a subject of historical action.

You will ask yourselves: what has caused this Latin American backwardness? Why, if we won political independence more or less at the same time, are North Americans prosperous, free, democratic—and Latin Americans poor, subjugated, unable to govern themselves? You will sigh with relief: now, everything is going to change, thanks to American generosity. The Alliance for Progress will solve all the problems afflicting Latin America. Thanks to those $20 billion, Latin Americans will forget the spectre of revolution so stained with blood and destructive of democracy and human rights, will manage to develop peacefully and, in a short time, will set up democratic societies, twins of the United States.

⇒    You are much given to good wishes, to what you call "wishful thinking." You have always believed that what is valid for you is valid for all men in all nations and at all times. You forget the existence of specific historical factors. You fail to realize that in reality there are two worlds, one of rich countries and one of poor countries. You fail to recognize that, of necessity, the poor countries require solutions different from yours. You have had four centuries of uninterrupted development within the capitalistic structure. We have had four centuries of underdevelopment within a feudal structure.

## A Feudal Castle with a Capitalistic Facade

You must understand this key word: *structure*. You had your own origin in the capitalistic revolution, liberal and Protestant. You were born without an anachronistic link. You founded a society that, from its first moment, was identified with the historical reason of the times. You created an economy directed towards the creation of wealth in the social vacuum of Anglo-Saxon America. You did not have to fight against and assimilate the resistance of local cultures. You started from zero, a virgin society, totally equal to modern times, without any feudal ballast. On the contrary, we were founded as an appendix of the falling feudal order of the Middle Ages; we inherited its obsolete structures, absorbed its vices, and converted them into institutions on the outer rim of the revolution in the modern world. If you come from the Reformation, we come from the Counter-Reformation: slavery to work, to religious dogmatism, to *latifundio* (enormous expanses of land under the same landlord), denial of political, economic, or cultural rights for the masses, a customs house closed to modern ideas. Instead of creating our own wealth, we exported it to the Spanish and Portuguese metropolis. When we obtained political independence, we did not obtain economic independence; the structure did not change.

You must understand that the Latin American drama stems from the persistence of those feudal structures over four centuries of misery and stagnation, while you were in the midst of the industrial revolution and were exercising a liberal democracy. You must understand that the only solution for Latin Americans will be to destroy all those structures at once.

But you ask yourselves: is a revolution necessary? Why not abolish those structures through evolution? The answer is simple: because the formulas of free-enterprise capitalism have already had their historical opportunity in Latin America and have proved unable to abolish feudalism.

During the nineteenth century, economic liberalism—laissez faire—was superimposed on the feudal structure in Latin America. Side by side with the landlord class of the colonial period, a new class of entrepreneurs sprang up to deal in the business of exploitation. Those capitalists turned us into single-product countries, exporters of raw materials to the occidental marketplace. The utopia of these entrepreneurs was the following: because of the international division of labor, it was appropriate for some regions to produce raw materials and for others to refine them; such an exchange would produce welfare for everyone. Now we know this is not true; now we know that, in the long run, the price of manufactured goods will always be higher than that of raw materials. Now we know that in a depression of the central economy, those who suffer most are the satellite economies, the producers of raw materials. Between 1929 and 1938, Latin American exports decreased by 70 percent. In that time, hunger *did* exist in Cuba: 50 percent of her labor force was unemployed, the national banks failed, the sugar lands were bought at bargain prices by Americans. The myth collapsed. If economies were complementary, as the classical theory states, our standard of living should be equal to yours.

In order to overcome the effects of economic liberalism, many Latin American countries entered another phase after 1930: protectionist capitalism, with the aim of encouraging the internal industrialization of Latin America and making it less dependent on the export of raw materials. But this naive and liberal capitalism was also superimposed on the feudal structure without destroying it. It abandoned to their fate the great masses of peasants and workers, and reserved progress for an urban minority. It ended by crystallizing a dual society in Latin

America: the modern capitalistic society of cities and the feudal society of the countryside. The minority society became richer at every turn, face-to-face with a majority society becoming more miserable at every turn. In the last few years, the abyss between the two has done nothing but grow. This is why capitalism has not succeeded in solving the problems of Latin America. It has been unable to destroy the legacy of feudalism. It has been unable to promote true collective development in Latin America.

This is what Latin America is: a collapsed feudal castle with a cardboard capitalistic facade.

This is the panorama of the historical failure of capitalism in Latin America:

— *Continuous monoproductive dependence*. In Brazil, coffee constitutes 74 percent of the exports; tin in Bolivia, 60 percent; copper in Chile, 63 percent; bananas in Costa Rica, 60 percent; coffee in Colombia, 82 percent; bananas in Honduras, 75 percent; coffee in Haiti, 63 percent; oil in Venezuela, 95 percent; coffee in Nicaragua, 51 percent; sugar in the Dominican Republic, 60 percent.

— *A continuous system of "latifundio."* In Chile and Brazil, 2 percent of the population owns 50 percent of the workable land. In Venezuela, 3 percent of the population owns 90 percent of the land. In general, in Latin America, with the exception of Mexico and Cuba, 5 percent of the population owns half of the land. More than half of all Latin Americans are peasants who work under conditions close to slavery. However, only 24 percent of the land in Latin America can be cultivated. Of this percentage, enormous expanses are out of active production, either to maintain the earnings of the owners or through pure irrationality. Most Latin American countries must import a good part of their food; only Uruguay and Argentina are relatively self-sufficient. The productivity of agriculture is extremely low in relation to the manpower employed. And international prices of the agricultural products fluctuate and are constantly declining.

— *Continuous underdevelopment*. The present systems are unable to increase production and use natural resources in the rhythm required by our increase in population. As a result, the average annual increase in production per inhabitant in Latin America which in 1955 was 2.2 percent, declined in 1959 to 1 percent, and in 1960 to 0.0 percent. In other words, at present, in its double feudal-capitalistic system, Latin America *does not progress.*

— *Continuous political stagnation.* The continued existence of the feudal structure forbids the masses access to education and assures the concentration of political power in the hands of a fistful of landlords and city capitalists. Latin American armies financed and equipped by the United States, support this system, as we have just seen in Argentina, Ecuador, and Guatemala.

— *Continous general injustices.* At present, 4 percent of the Latin American population receives 50 percent of the combined national incomes. The higher classes have hoarded more than 14 billion dollars in foreign banks. A great percentage of their local investments are unproductive ones: fixed-income securities, real estate, luxury goods.

— *Continuous dependence on foreign capital.* At present, a good part of the Latin American economy is not serving its own development, but is nothing more than an extension of foreign economies, particularly that of the United States. Iron and oil in Venezuela, copper in Chile, Peruvian minerals, do not remain in those countries to promote economic development: they are a possession of the American economy and benefit only that economy. But since this is a topic very closely related to you, we will talk about it later.

The key question is this: How can the causes of underdevelopment in Latin America be chopped away? There is no room for doubt in the answer: stabilization of prices of raw materials in the short run, and economic diversification—industrialization—in the long run. But you want it to be done through peaceful evolution and the Alliance for Progress. And we think: through revolution. Let us examine both solutions.

## The Alliance for Progress

The only structural reform foreseen in the Alliance for Progress is agrarian reform. Now, please consider that in Latin America the base of political power is the landlords. Do you sincerely believe that a leading class whose roots are in the ownership of land is going to let go of its reason for being? Agrarian feudalism is the basis of the wealth and political dominion of the governing classes in Central America, Chile, Peru, Argentina, Brazil, Venezuela, Colombia, Ecuador; do you believe these classes are going to commit suicide voluntarily? A Peruvian oligarch recently told me: "If the gringos force us to divide the land, we will answer by expropriating their mining companies." No, my American friends: an agrarian reform in Latin America, as demonstrated by Mexico and Cuba, is only made through revolution, with weapons in hand. This is what the sharecroppers of Peru, the peasants of northeastern Brazil, the pariahs of Chile, Ecuador, and Colombia are beginning to do. They are not allowing themselves to be cheated by "false" agrarian reforms: the distribution of sterile lands, without credit, without machinery, without schools or hospitals. Those governing classes can deceive you, but they are not going to swindle the peasant masses or stifle their revolutionary impetus.

The Alliance is going to be used by governments that do not truly represent their people, by governments representing the old feudal order whose only interest is to keep its privileges. Look where your dollars are going to go: as in South Vietnam, as in South Korea, as in Iran and Spain—to the bank accounts of a handful of people, to the importation of luxurious automobiles, to the construction of apartment houses.

The Alliance does not even mention one of the basic factors of backwardness in Latin America: the economic deformation imposed by foreign domination of our economies. Ah, you jump at this point. You refuse to admit this. You have helped the development (what development?) of Latin America. You unselfishly give us dollars and technical aid.

We have already spoken about the domination of natural resources: iron ore, copper, tin, coal, lead, zinc, oil. These resources, in your hands, enter your economy: they are not employed in the internal development of our countries. The Alliance does not even speak of that. It does not foresee that the iron and oil of Venezuela may contribute to creation of heavy industry there, that the copper of Chile or the lead of Peru may be motors of national industrialization. At any rate, our industrialization must be light, for transformation, but nothing more.

You are also proprietors of Latin American foreign trade. Sixty percent of our foreign trade is with you, in accordance with the prices you set. American companies manage 75 percent of our commercial movement. You impose the conditions and the prices. Last year, the Alliance gave 150 million dollars to Colombia; but in that same year, Colombia lost 450 million dollars because of the decrease in coffee prices.

Ask the great cotton concerns how much they pay for a bale of Mexican cotton, at what price they resell it to the English monopoly in Hong Kong, and how much they charge the Communist government of China, which you detest, for it. The Anderson Clayton in this operation makes five times the amount that the Mexican grower does. And ask the Department of State why it forbids Mexico to sell its excess oranges to Czechoslovakia in exchange for machinery we need, machinery you either do not sell us or sell us for too high a price; ask the Department why the whole crop went rotten on the docks of Tampico while you traded happily with Communist countries and allowed Adenauer's Germany to be the principal Western market of that very same Czechoslovakia.

Investments? Yes, you have invested 10 billion dollars in Latin America. It is a curious thing: we have always received your investments, and we are still poor. You speak about *your* property in Latin America and call us thieves when we expropriate it. But why don't you ask your investors? Ask them how much they invest and how much they take back to the United States in profits. Do you want to know? Between 1950 and 1955, you invested 2 billion dollars, made three and a half billion, and took back to the States one and a half billion. In a single year, 1959, you made 775 million, only reinvested 200 million and sent 575 million back to the United States. In the last 7 years, Latin America lost, because of these shipments of money, $2,679,000,000. You take out too much, leave too little, and even this little is distributed unfairly: where is the real benefit for our economies? Is it just that these profits do nothing, not a single thing, to alleviate the horrible misery, ignorance, and illness of the great majority of the Latin Americans who, with their slavery, made them possible? You, as Americans, tell me if that is just.

And tell me also whether you have not recovered more than your investments, whether it is not right that this squandered wealth should be recovered and directed towards improving the lot of everyone, because it was created by the work of everyone though today it benefits only a dozen corporations.

Finally, in its year of life, the Alliance for Progress has been accompanied by acts of political aggression that prostitute it completely. These acts are the Cuban invasion in April, 1961, and the violation of the inter-American law in Punta del Este in January, 1962.

## Playa Giron and Punta del Este

American responsibility in the invasion of the Bay of Pigs is not debatable: President Kennedy assumed it completely, with full knowledge that in this way he was violating not only inter-American treaties but the internal laws of the United States itself: the Neutrality Act and the U.S. Code. You pride yourselves on living in a State of Law. Why did you allow your government to violate it? Don't you count on representatives of the people to defend it? Is there not a process to call to account —impeach—the president who violates it? Why do you permit an apparently irrational act by your government, your CIA and a band of mercenaries recruited from the assassins and sadists of the Batista government? Or do you agree with your government in considering the law a dead letter when faced by political necessities? In this case you yourselves are justifying Goldwater, the John Birch Society, and all the fascist forces that, beginning with McCarthy, have been growing in the United States of America.

You killed women and children in Playa Giron. You bombed the first decent houses, the first schools, the first hospitals of Cubans who never before, during the long American protectorate over Cuba, had a roof, an alphabet, or their health. And you did it in the name of liberty, democracy, and free enterprise. What do you want us to think of these nice-sounding words when in their names a population is murdered and the first proofs of concrete welfare are destroyed? We think the same as Simon Bolivar did 150 years ago: "The U.S.A. seems destined by Providence to plague us with all kinds of evils in the name of liberty."

In Punta del Este, the second agressive act in the name of the Alliance took place. Maybe for you the standards of inter-American law are not important, but for us they are the result of a long struggle. It took us a whole century to win these standards. We won them with the invasion of Mexico and the annexation of half our territory, with the mutilation of Colombia, with the Platt Amendment, with the murder of Madero, with the occupation of Veracruz and the punitive Pershing expedition, with the interventions in Haiti, Nicaragua, and Santo Domingo, with the death of Sandino, with the campaign and the pressure against the Mexican Revolution, with the violation of Guatemala. It cost us a great deal of blood to set these standards: self-determination, non-intervention, respect for territorial integrity, equal rights for natives and foreigners, peaceful solutions of controversies, the right of each American state to organize as it thinks best. In Punta del Este, all these standards were violated by your government. A century of judicial construction collapsed. It does not matter, said Secretary Rusk: "It is not the role of foreign ministers to discuss judicial matters, but to make decisions in the field of politics." The OAS ceased to be a legal organization because it was converted, now without any disguise, into a political weapon of the United States of America.

And the Alliance for Progress looked like the soft loincloth of naked intervention in favor of the concrete political and economic interest of the United States in Latin America.

### Revolution, Yes

For years, many Latin Americans put faith in a gradual change of American policies towards Latin America; they also put their faith in the ability of the inter-American organization to support the minimum principles of our sovereignty. It is necessary to thank President Kennedy who, in only a year, has destroyed those illusions. The New Frontier turned out to be identical to the Republican Old Guard. Today, Latin Americans know they must no longer trust in the possibility of a change in the American government or in the OAS: they must trust only in themselves, in their capacity to destroy, by themselves, the old feudal structure and replace it with a radically new society, from which they can build for themselves.

Revolution? Yes, because as Mexico and Cuba have demonstrated, only revolution, not aspirins or good wishes, can destroy feudalism.

Revolution? Yes, because as Mexico and Cuba have demonstrated, only armed revolution can destroy forever the armies of caste, protectors of the old order. Or do you believe that the army which has just annulled the will of the people and deposed the constitutional president in Argentina is going to disappear voluntarily from the political scene? Do you think it just that this Argentine army, with more officers than the American army, is devouring 50 percent of the national budget? And do you think it just, as taxpayers, that your money should go to equip these caste armies? With your money, these armies prepare revolts, murder workers, torture students, and void elections.

— Revolution? Yes, because as Mexico and Cuba have demonstrated, only revolution can produce the structural changes necessary to modernize our countries, get our stagnant resources moving, resources that were sold and squandered, realize agrarian reform, create an internal market, diversify production, promote popular education, and push industrialization.

Revolution! You cry to heaven, wring your hands, weep before violence and bloodletting. Yes. Unfortunately, it has never been possible to persuade the leading classes of a feudal country that their last hour has come. The Count of Arana, in the eighteenth century, could not persuade them, and President Kennedy, in the twentieth, cannot either. Porfirio Diaz and Fulgencio Batista were convinced only at gunpoint. This is the only way the Peruvian landlords, the Argentine militarists, and the Colombian landlords are going to be convinced. Blood? Yes, historical backwardness is paid for in blood. Injustice is paid for in blood. Remember Jefferson. From Spartacus to Fidel Castro, going through the Protestant, English, French, American, Mexican, and Russian Revolutions, revolutions have been accomplished by violence. Mickey Mouse does not make revolutions. They are made by hungry men, valiant, angry, desperate men.

But you complain: what about democracy and liberty? Why, instead of bringing representative democracy, human rights, elections and a free press, do Latin American revolutions impose a leftist dictatorship in the place of a deposed rightist dictatorship? Why do they impose a single party, start a wave of political emigrants, suppress freedom of the press and elections? Why do they invite the protection of extra-continental powers?

Ah, this is what is worrying you. This is what you do not understand. You should start remembering. You have a very bad memory. You would do well to remember your own revolution in the eighteenth century. You also had your traitors, your deserters, and your execution walls. Like all revolutions, yours begot a counter-revolution. In those times, you had 3,500,000 inhabitants; 70,000 fled the United States to find shelter in Canada. You expropriated the belongings and lands of exiled people without paying them anything. You suppressed the pro-British press. You won the revolution with the help of a foreign power, France. Without Rochambeau's French troops and De Grasse's fleet, you could not have defeated the British. You suffered shameful press campaigns, were labeled "bandits and savages" by the royal European press. You used "exotic doctrines"—those of the French encyclopedists—to form a republican government, a heresy against the status quo imposed and defended by the Holy Alliance. You were the devils, the heretics, the non-conformists of the eighteenth century. You had to resist the counter-revolutionary invasion of 1812, your own Playa Giron, with Andrew Jackson's improvised militia. But you, during the colonial period, had already practiced representative democracy. You did not live under feudalism; you were already Protestants and capitalists; you were not struggling along as an exploited, illiterate hungry mass of people.

In our day, a true revolution in Latin America is equivalent to a war of independence. It means starting from the bottom and creating conditions that, at least, will permit the exercise of democracy. A democracy cannot exist, you know, with empty stomachs, empty minds, and empty shacks. Democracy is not a cause; it is a result.

Sacrificing democracy through revolution? Not if there has never been democracy in Latin America. It has been democracy solely of paper and rhetoric. Sacrificing elections? Not if elections in Latin America have been only a ceremony and a fraud. Sacrificing human rights? Which ones? Those of men who do not eat, do not read, do not write, who live in humiliation and terror? Sacrificing freedom of the press? Not if there is no such thing in Latin America; there is an anti-national corrupt press at the service of the interests of feudalism and the most powerful foreign nation at hand.

No, the problem is different. The revolution would bring to power the popular majority that for centuries has had neither voice nor votes. In the eyes of this majority, the corrupt press, fraudulent elections, submission to foreigners, freedom of enterprise and the human rights of the minority that oppressed the majority are synonyms of those centuries of exploitation, of negation, of not being. This is not what the people are interested in. They are interested in *concrete* democracy: the starting point of their real aspirations. They are interested in destroying the old structure of exploitations; they are interested in creating their own new structures, national, popular, with collective benefits, in the knowledge that many mistakes will be committed and many failures endured, but with the hope that this time they will be working for themselves and for their future and not for a bunch of feudal landlords and foreign enterprises. Of course, this transformation demands great sacrifices and is not easy to bring about: four centuries of insanity weigh against it. But there is no other way. The only available alternative is to bear, forever, the old injustice.

Can't you understand this? Why do you seem so hysterical, so jealous, so angry when a revolution puts into action the liberated energies of the people, and why so indifferent, so calm, so thoughtful when these same people are exploited, tyrannized, and debased by a feudal oligarchy? Why did you not start press campaigns against Somoza, why did you not invade Venezuela while Perez Jimenez was in power, why did you support Trujillo for 30 years, why have you not declared yourselves against Stroessner? What do you want us to think when you have supported and still support regimes of corruption and crime, but fling yourselves against regimes of honesty and work: against Cuba?

However, it no longer matters what you do or do not do. We already know the path. Open your eyes. Today it is Cuba. Tomorrow. . . . Keep your eyes open. The armies of privilege will be defeated. The old structures will collapse. Land, mines, businesses will be recovered. They will work for the benefit of everyone. There will be difficulties of conversion and organization. But in the long run the economy will be diversified, idle land will be cultivated, illiteracy will be eradicated, the liberated farmer's consumption of goods will increase, national resources will be used for national industrialization, culture will also belong to workers and farmers, and decent houses, hospitals, highways, and schools will be built.

Is this a dream? No, it is not. This is our challenge. Feudalism and superimposed capitalism have failed, in four centuries, to achieve any of this. You said that nationalization of oil was a daydream in Mexico; that within a year the foreign companies would be back because Mexicans were unable to manage such a complex industry. You were right: we *were* unable to do it, we had many difficult moments, just as difficult as those Cuba is now having. But with time, as is happening with Cuba, we created our technicians, our specialized workers, and we succeeded, we surpassed the old companies in efficiency and now we use our oil for our own benefit, rationally. We will not forget this experience: where the Latin American man becomes owner of his land, his industry, his work, he pulls himself out of the ineptitude of past centuries and shows what he can do. This is going to happen, don't you doubt it, in the next few years in Latin America. Nobody learns to swim without diving into the water.

Revolution, yes! ! Don't be deceived, Americans. Open your eyes. Ask the Peruvian farmer who chews coca and eats rats if he wants fake elections or revolutions. Ask the Chilean miner who crawls through the tunnels of Lota if he believes in free enterprise or in revolution. Ask the northeast Brazilian farmer if he wants capitalism or revolution. Ask the student castrated by the Paraguayan dictator if he wants Stroessner's free press or revolution. Ask the Guatemalan farmer "freed" by Castillo Armas if he wants Alliance for Progress or revolution. Ask the Latin Americans who corrupts the press and the unions, who supports the armies and the oligarchies, who pays miserable salaries, who owns the mines and the oil wells. Ask them who gets the Alliance for Progress money, and ask what they use it for. Ask them if we believe in the free world of Franco, Salazar, Chiang-Kai-shek and Ngo Dinh Diem. Ask them and they will tell you why people spat on Nixon.

Ask the men living in "misery village" in Buenos Aires, in the "favela" of Rio, in the "cayampa population" of Santiago, if they are afraid of Communism. These beggars, these pariahs, will answer that they are afraid only of their present oppressors, of those who exploit them in the name of capitalism and representative democracy, and that they prefer anything that might mean a change.

Ask these men if they are against Cuba, if they believe the lies they read in the "free press" of our countries, if they do not know that the old American colony of the Caribbean is our hope because there the caste army, the *latifundio,* the administrative corruption, the official cheating are over and everybody works together, with weapons ready, Americans, with weapons ready to defend the Revolution; tell Ydigoras or Somoza to arm their people with the weapons you give them— and then to move forward together despite aggression and boycott.

Ask these men if they are afraid of help from the Soviet Union. Ask them if there is a single Soviet company in Cuba that exploits the Cuban economy for its own gain.

Do you see, Americans? The world has changed. Latin America is no longer your preserve. The world moves ahead. And you are standing on the rim. Are you going to help these inevitable revolutions or are you going to antagonize them with invasions, press campaigns, and economic aggressions? It does not matter. Revolutions are going to progress. The world has changed. You will not be able to put out all the fires in Latin America, Africa, and Asia.

But try to understand. Try to understand that a revolution in Latin America can affect only a handful of Yankee enterprises, but never the concrete welfare you enjoy. Try to understand that our real development, which can be achieved only through revolution, far from hurting you will help you. Do not let yourselves be fooled by this handful of enterprises and investors. Try to understand that the sooner we start our basic development, which can come only through revolution, the more buyers you will have, and we will all be closer to a planned world economy, rational and interdependent.

## What We Want

Understand this: Latin America is not going to be your back yard any more. We are going to enter the world. What kind of world?

Apparently, a world characterized by the political polarization of two power centers: the United States and the Soviet Union, facing one another from unchangeable positions—but both limited by the knowledge that a "hot war" will end not with victor and vanquished but with the total destruction of the human race.

But behind this obvious factor there is now another one: the upsurge of the underdeveloped countries and the possibility that they may dissolve this polarization, diversify and rationalize the international political positions, and confront the world with the primary job of peace—to cooperate in the economic and social development of those underdeveloped countries. The Soviet Union, as much as it can, is already doing so. And you? The first measure of cooperation is to know how to respect the revolutionary change that is taking place in those countries.

And there is a third factor, of truly universal perspective: over and above the visible conflicts of our world, there is emerging the development of modern science and the opportunity it offers to all men, without any distinction of political ideology, religious belief, sex, or race, to achieve a truly human life, free from illness, ignorance, and hunger and full of promise for personal and collective creation. Please, try to see beyond the intellectual provincialism of the cold war. Try to see where we want to arrive, we men of the underdeveloped world, hungry, revolutionary. We do not want the destruction of the American people, which we love for the expressions of its great people, its great political names—Lincoln, Franklin Roosevelt—and artistic names—Poe, Melville, Faulkner, Marian Anderson, O'Neill, Miller. We do not want atomic hatred, or a permanent cold war, but a world of peace in which we may grow without anachronistic deformations, without irrational exploitations. We want a world in which everyone coexists, not in mutual tolerance but in mutual respect and friendship.

We are different from you. Our problems are not your problems. We have to make decisions and walk on roads different from those you believe to be universally valid. Do not be provincial. Try to understand the diversity of the world. Try to understand we want progress that is real, not the unjust lie of today. We want *to be*. We want to live with you as loyal friends, not as sick, poorly fed, ignorant slaves. We want a rational organization of development in which science can, at least, distribute its fruits universally. We want to arrive at a peaceful synthesis of oppositions that are not, nor can ever be, eternal, any more than those of Greeks and Romans, Roman and barbarians, Guelphs and Ghibellines, Catholics and Protestants, monarchists and republicans, were. We want to be free of slavery, and we want to save you from a destiny worse than that of the slave: that of the lord, of the master.

Latin America knows its own path. Nobody, my American friends, is going to stop those 200 million people.

# THE PLUNDERED CONTINENT

## BY PAUL JOHNSON

The following is an abridgment of an article which appeared in the London *New Statesman* of September 17, 1960. Mr. Johnson is one of the editors of the *New Statesman*. His vivid description of conditions in the main South American countries should be enough to convince even the most hard-boiled imperialist that United States policy, aimed as it is at maintaining the status quo in Latin America, is failing and is bound to fail. By the same token, Mr. Johnson's article helps to explain the tremendous impact of the Cuban Revolution throughout Latin America. To avoid misunderstanding, it should be added that we are not convinced, as Mr. Johnson appears to be, that Brazil can successfully develop on a capitalist basis in the second half of the 20th century as the United States did in the second half of the 19th century. There are, it seems to us, decisive differences, both internal and international, between the two cases. Apart from this one point, however, we are in general agreement with Mr. Johnson's analysis.—The Editors

Latin America might have been the kingdoms of the world the Devil showed Christ on the mountain. It has more cultivable, high yield tropical soil than any other continent, at least three times as much agricultural land, per capita, as Asia, the biggest reserves of timber in the world. Buried in it are uncalculated but vast reserves of oil, iron, copper, tin, gold, silver, zinc, lead: the list is endless—it embraces virtually every metal, base and rare, and every industrial chemical known to man. With its oil and hydroelectric power it constitutes one of the greatest untapped reservoirs of energy; its annual population increase, hovering between two and three percent, provides an inexhaustible source of future manpower.

Yet Latin America contains some of the poorest and most exploited people on the planet. Its impact on world politics, over nearly 500 years, has been negligible. It has remained a rich and plundered flotsam, drifting on the rival tides of European and North American avarice.

Will it always be like this? Will Latin America remain the plundered continent? Or is the time coming when its peoples will step onto the world stage in their own right, and play the massive part to which their economic wealth entitles them? These were the questions I set myself and tried to answer during a 30,000-mile voyage through this area.

My trip began, logically, in Brazil: for the first half of the answer depends upon the speed at which Brazil's experiment in capitalist economics comes to maturity. It ended, again logically, in Cuba: for the success of the present political experiment there is the necessary compliment to the Brazilian upsurge. In examining these two questions, we shall find ourselves touching upon virtually all the problems of the continent.

Superficially, Brazil is just another Latin American state. Its per capita income is among the lowest on the continent. Between 60 and 75 percent—no-one seems to know—of Brazilians are illiterate; even in Rio State, the proportion is over half. Only 5 percent of the cultivable land is under crops. It has a tiny, ramshackle railway network with less mileage than Belgium, but five different gauges and 29 different systems; most of the engines burn wood, which has to be transported long distances by lorries consuming imported petrol. To a great extent, it still has a one-crop economy, with all the attendant evils. Half the population scarcely handles money and cannot afford to buy manufactured goods. In the northeast, when the drought comes, the inhabitants—they are called *flagelados,* those who are whipped—live off cactus. There's no color prejudice, true; it's just that the Negroes, still less the Indians, don't seem to get very far. The army and navy are well looked after. Government, as in 18th-century England, is a branch of private enterprise. The police mind their own business, unless attacked. About half the country is unexplored, three-quarters unvisited by respectable citizens. Since the collapse of the rubber boom, there's no point in going near the Amazon; no way of getting there, either, unless you want to chug up it in verminous boats, or risk a flight across 1,000 miles of jungle. This, at any rate, is the picture you get in Rio, where hope is a stunted plant, wedged between the most villainous slums in the world and the flagrant evidence of unprincipled wealth.

In Sao Paulo, it's a different story. Unlike Rio, the city has escaped from the debilitating frustrations of the coast, which turns longing eyes back towards Europe. It is in the center of the *terra roxa,* the rich red earth which grows the world's best coffee. Unlike all other Latin American cities, it is not an artificial creation, an ant-hill refuge for men beaten by the land. It has sprung up as a natural process of economic growth: efficient farming led to the creation of agricultural surpluses; these in turn produced capital; capital was invested in industry, selling its products to rich farmers and salaried laborers. Suddenly, in the last quarter of the 19th century, the process began to reach maturity, and Sao Paulo exploded. From a population of 25,000 in 1875, it has expanded to nearly four million, and is growing at the rate of 150,000 a year. It spreads over 700 square miles, virtually without slums. The centre is a vast canyon of roads, lipped by the biggest skyscrapers in the southern hemisphere; around, stretch pleasant residential suburbs, occupied—and in Latin America this is a miracle—by ordinary bank clerks and industrial workers. For, if Sao Paulo boasts of its 100 million-aires, it also has something which is economically far more significant: a million and a half regular wage-earners—the vital atoms of a modern consumer economy.

For this is the real importance of Sao Paulo. Within the city and in the rich agricultural and industrial hinterland are some 12 to 15 million people who have decisively crossed the subsistence threshold. In the past in Brazil, and elsewhere in Latin America even today, economic growth is paralysed by a total dependence on overseas markets. Manufactured imports could only be paid for by exporting raw materials—food and minerals. The people were tied to the land, leading a subsistence economy; and any investment in the land meant overproduction, price collapses, and unemployment. Local industry died of inanition: nobody could afford to buy the goods. There seemed no way out of this vicious circle.

Now Sao Paulo has broken it, for good. The slow process of natural agricultural growth has created a reservoir of consumers. These have been joined by what economists call "high-grade" immigrants—1,250,000 Italians, 1,000,000 Portuguese, 400,000 Spaniards, 250,000 Japanese, 100,000 Lebanese and Syrians—bringing with them capital, energy, and industrial skills which cannot be purchased south of the Rio Grande. As a result, the area has an annual consumer purchasing power of over $15,000 million—the basis for self-sustaining growth.

The problem now has entered a new phase. How, operating from its solidly established base in Sao Paulo, can this new wealth "colonize" the rest of Brazil? Until a few years ago, the problem seemed insoluble: distance, sheer physical difficulties, and the prevailing inertia elsewhere were tending to turn Sao Paulo in upon itself. Now, by forcing through the construction of Brasilia, President Kubitschek has broken Rio's palsied grip upon government and built a psychological as well as a physical bridge across which Sao Paulo's wealth can flow to the interior and the north. Now the emphasis is no longer on direction, but solely on speed.

In Brazil's present stage of evolution, such terms as socialism are meaningless. The country resembles the United States during the great westward surge of the mid-19th century. I found a complete absence of interest in the outside world, an avid self-absorption in the immediate business of making money. This national climate may be disagreeable; but it is healthy and necessary. Unlike the rest of Latin America, there is little self-pity in Brazil. Violence, yes; poverty, the vicious cruelty of glaring economic inequality. But no doubts about the future. Before the end of the century, Brazil will have a population of 200 million. It will be the biggest industrial power south of the equator, playing a giant's role in the world. The type of economic and political regime it will then possess can and must be left to the next generation to decide.

In Brazil, hope; in the rest of the continent resignation, even despair. This sweeping generalization is a useful rule of thumb south of Panama.

Vast, sprawling Buenos Aires (it numbers 5 million, with a further 2 million in the outer suburbs), once so elegant, with its cherished echoes of Paris, now has a down-at-heel, second-hand air. The street lights splutter on and off at night, there are great, unfilled cavities in the pavements, peeling plaster on the public buildings.

The postwar history of Argentina is an unmitigated tragedy. It also epitomizes all the main problems which face Latin American countries, apart from Brazil. After Venezuela, whose wealth springs almost entirely from oil, it has the highest per capita income in the area and by far the highest literacy rate.

The British provided it with the biggest railway network south of the equator and the elements of an industrial base. What went wrong? Briefly, Argentina's troubles spring from Peron's clumsy but well-meaning attempts to make it economically and industrially independent. This desire for release from the foreigner is present throughout Latin America. For a time, in the rosy postwar era of high commodity prices, it seemed as though Argentina might realize it.

Basing his power on organized labor, Peron's dream was to convert Argentina from an agricultural into an industrial country—the powerhouse of the continent. Excessive world demand for beef and grain gave him a vast exchange surplus during the forties. He used this to buy out foreign investments—to the tune of nearly $400 million—and to force through a state program of rapid industrialization. He also used export exchange rates to penalize agriculture. Inevitably, food production fell dramatically, exports dwindled, the rural workers poured into the cities in search of high, artificially-fixed wages, imports rose—not only for industry but for the swollen rural populations—and the economy swung into a vicious inflationary spin. This crackpot experiment was doomed in any case; but the collapse of world commodity prices in the 1950's turned it into disaster. Argentina's food exports were falling in quantity at precisely the time when their value was collapsing. The economy came to a virtual stop: by 1955, the gross national product was over seven percent lower than in 1948. After a few half-hearted efforts to reverse the process, the Peron regime collapsed in a maelstrom of bloodshed and police tyranny.

Peron left a fearful legacy. It is axiomatic in Latin America that once you have dragged a peasant off the land into the city, you can never get him back again, no matter how poor he is. It is also axiomatic that no Latin American government can be induced to take a serious interest in agriculture. Hence production of Argentina's real wealth—cattle and grain—remains static. Three quarters of the population live in the towns eating their heads off (in one year, the country even had to import wheat). Because Peronist memories still linger among the urban workers, the government dare not allow wages to find their market level: so industry remains hopelessly uncompetitive and stagnant. Nearly everyone is underemployed. The sprawling, state-owned railways (run at a gigantic loss) have, I was told, 75 percent surplus personnel. Nearly 14 percent of the work force is employed by government; and, short of a revolution, nobody can be fired from a government office.

What, in these circumstances, can any government do? President Frondizi and his Intransigent Radicals were elected on a violently left-wing platform with Peronist support. He pledged himself to carry out what Peron had manifestly failed to do; once in office, he found this was impossible. Inflation was proceeding at a steady trot of 50 percent a year; external payments were in permanent unbalance; it was out of the question to salvage the wreck of the industrialization program without a massive injection of foreign capital—and where was that to come from? Short of imposing a Communist dictatorship, and beating the country into raising itself by its bootstraps, Frondizi had only one choice: to sell the country, lock, stock and barrel, to the United States.

This, in effect, is what he has done, but in a subtle, mid-20th century way. The U.S. bankers of the International Monetary Fund have made available initial credits of $329 million, on condition that the government follows an economic policy of which they approve. This means, in practice, savage deflation, euphemized under the title of the Stabilization Program. A dramatic fall in consumption, unemployment, wage cuts, strikes, police action have followed in inevitable progression. The country is unhappy and uncertain. Moreover, to date, Frondizi's policy seems to be failing on all counts. He has not dared to take the political risks of dismantling sufficient of the protective and paternalist legal machinery of Peronism to make his new policy work; but at the same time he has made himself just sufficiently unpopular to become absolutely dependent on the army. This is now the real ruler of the country. Just before I arrived there, parliament was forced, virtually at pistol point, to hand over the state of Cordoba to military rule. The army now controls the Ministry of the Interior, and has reimposed the death penalty for terrorism—i.e., attacks on officers. Parts of the country are now in a state of incipient anarchy. Armed bands roam the pampas. Time bombs explode in railway stations. Trade unionists and journalists are savagely beaten in secret police stations. Under the nominal aegis of a left-wing democratically elected government, Argentina today bears all the hallmarks of Franco Spain: industrial stagnation, rising unemployment, inflation, and police terror.

Unfortunately, the recent history of Argentina finds echoes all over the continent. With varying degrees of violence, the same pattern can be traced, in Chile, in Peru, in Venezuela, for example. The origins of this continental *malaise* can be traced back to the Spanish *conquistadors*. It is impossible to be too critical of this mindless bunch of ruffians. Their principal aim, as they hacked their way up and down the Pacific Coast, was to get their hands on gold or other precious metals. Failing this, they looked for large concentrations of Indians, who could be turned into slave laborers on cash-crop farms. In an astonishingly short period, they wrecked not only one of the most complex agricultural civilizations in history, but the very earth itself. The Inca empire in Peru had supported 30 million people in material abundance; its wealth was based on scientific strip contour farming, kept efficient by an elaborate bureaucracy. Despite the absence of either the wheel or the horse, communications were better (taking the country as a whole) than in present-day Peru: the great ravines were spanned by superb bridges of wood and rope, kept in excellent repair.

This inheritance the Spaniards threw away in the blind pursuit of easy wealth. Some of the Indians were dragged down from the Andean plateau to die on the tropical farms of the coast; others were dragged up from the coast to die in the mines. The bridges were used until they collapsed: the story of the bridge of San Luis Rey is symbolic of the whole colonial period. With the death of the Indians, the rich terraces were abandoned. I travelled hundreds of miles through the great Peruvian valleys. Everywhere, in the midst of the raw, desolate landscape, were the faint scratchings which marked what had once been a wonder of husbandry. Instead, the Spaniards pillaged the plains: agricultural plunder at its crudest. A forest was burnt down, crops sown; after a few years, when the soil began to fail, the Spaniards moved on and burnt another forest. Stripped of its forest cover, the soil was washed into the sea by the torrential Andean rains, or scattered into desert by the high winds. In the sea, the soil turned into sludge and poisoned the inshore fisheries. In Colombia, Ecuador, Chile—all down the Pacific coast—it is the same story of senseless plunder, the same rapid conversion of priceless, irreplaceable natural wealth into desert.

The only restrictions on the appetites of the Spanish *colons,* the only forces which could prevent them from wiping out the Indians entirely and finally destroying the continent's resources, were the Spanish crown and the church. The crown, in its fumbling way, tried to operate conservation policies and even imposed laws against killing Indians wholesale. The church was more positive. Some of the missionaries, notably the Jesuits, set up inland colonies, farming the land on scientific principles, resurrecting native handicrafts, trying to recreate in a beaten race the sense of human dignity. As such, they became mortal enemies of the *colons,* and in the last decades of the 18th century they were hounded out. Their colonies, in Paraguay and northern Argentina, can still be seen: crumbling, overgrown churches, in superb rococo, the patterns of once-rich fields. In turn, the feeble efforts of the crown to impose reason proved too irksome. Around 1820, the territories, one by one, rejected the authority of Spain and set up aristocratic republics.

The revolutions were essentially *colon* uprisings against the restrictive humanitarianism of the central power. As such, they find a modern echo in Algeria. But in 1820, General Massu —in the person of Bolivar, San Martin and the rest—flew the White Ensign. For it was the British Navy, holding the ring while the insurgents smashed the Spanish garrisons, which made the republican triumph possible. More than this, British capital, avid to break the Spanish monopoly and thrust its way into the rich investment territories of the continent, played an active role in financing revolt. The British government provided diplomatic backing. Canning was the Krushchev of the 1820's. It was a legion of Peninsula veterans, recruited from the London slums, which enabled Bolivar to free Venezuela and plunge across the Andes into Colombia. British gold financed San Martin. Admiral Cochrane transported his forces up the Pacific coast. Once Spanish rule had collapsed, the officers and *colons* turned on the Indians. In Argentina, San Martin's lieutenants massacred them to a man, and carved up the pampas into giant estates. In turn, the British moved into the ports and set up the great commercial and mining dynasties. The second age of plunder had begun. In the south and along the Pacific it was the British preserve; the Caribbean, the Isthmus, and Mexico was the American commercial empire, built by private armies and bribes, pocket presidents, gunboats, and marines.

Hence by the early years of the 20th century, Latin America had acquired its present characteristics. In virtually every country, a one-commodity economy (coffee, bananas, sugar, tin, or copper), tragically vulnerable to fluctuations in world prices. A socially and technically retrograde land system. Rule by small oligarchies, with over-large armed forces playing the role of arbiter and acting as a check on the normal functioning of the democratic system. Constant intervention by the great commercial powers.

How to escape from this complementary dominance of overseas commercial interests and internal feudal oligarchies has always been, and remains, the central problem for Latin American nationalists. The parallel with the Arab world is close: for there also an alien power (Turkey) had been usurped by western commerce, acting in conjunction with local, reactionary aristocrats. In Latin America, it has not proved particularly difficult, in recent times, for left-wing nationalists to win office through free elections; their problem has been how to win real power. In the smaller territories, such as Guatemala, legal governments can easily be overthrown by external intervention, sponsored by threatened commercial interests. Even in larger countries, such as Mexico and Bolivia, defiance of the foreigner can prove too costly. The Mexican oil industry is still being "punished" for nationalization: the international oil companies responded by building up the Venezuelan oil industry, just as in the Middle East they built up Kuwait to "punish" Persia. In Bolivia, the nationalized tin industry is starved of the capital required to make it competitive.

We have seen what happens when even a comparatively rich and technically advanced country like Argentina attempts to make itself master of its own economic destiny. It simply ends

by falling victim to the new type of colonizer—the cold-eyed
bankers in Washington. Today, the process can be observed at
work in a number of other Latin American regions. The jack-
booted foreign overseer has been succeeded by the Export-Import Bank economist in the grey flannel suit. To be sure, his
intentions are far more honorable than his predecessor's. What
the United States wants from Latin America is simply to be able
to extract or buy its raw materials—at what now begins to
approach a fair price—in an atmosphere of stable politics and
orthodox economics. It is able to get the type of government
which can provide these by offering—or withholding—large-
scale loans, without which Latin America cannot industrialize
at all. Washington hopes—genuinely, no doubt—that this atmosphere will, by some process of capitalist alchemy, produce
"healthy," regular, and eventually self-sustaining economic
growth, in a framework of monetary stability. Unfortunately,
neither growth nor stability has been, or is likely to be, achieved.
For political stability itself prevents the drastic changes in the
social and economic system which alone can provide the basis
for dynamic growth.

Chile is an example of this vicious circle in motion. In her
postwar efforts to get her industrial system off the ground,
Chile fell into a quagmire of inflation, inevitably accompanied
by a foreign-exchange crisis. The whole country is now in pawn
to the U.S.-dominated financial agencies—IMF, World Bank,
Export-Import Bank, etc.—who supply medium-sized loans in
return for the right to dictate financial policy to President
Alessandri's highly conservative government. The massive de-
flationary dose on which they insisted has merely depressed the
Chilean economy further. Industrial production fell 12 percent
between 1956 and 1958 and still seems to be falling; even
"official" unemployment is about 9 percent. Chile has all the
characteristics of a backward country. Income tax is a mere
3 and one-half percent (even so, there is at least 25 percent
evasion). Official interest rates are about 16 percent, with free
rates running up to 140 percent! Over 25 percent of the revenue
goes on the armed forces and police. Average real wages have
declined sharply since 1948, while real national income per
capita fell by 10 percent. Some 25 percent of the population—

whose real wealth comes almost entirely from land and minerals
—form a grossly inflated white-collar class, whose real wages
are rising rapidly at the expense of the productive workers. These
retrograde tendencies have all become more acute since the
U.S. bankers took over; at the same time, they have not even
succeeded in their basic objective—monetary stability. Inflation
jogs along at an average annual 20 percent clip, and my grubby
Chilean currency was looked at with suspicion even in Lima.

What, of course, is wrong with Chile is the legacy of the
*conquistadors,* the besetting and perennial sin of Latin America:
neglect of the land. Sao Paulo and Brazil have shown—as did
Britain in the 18th century—that self-sustaining economic growth
can be constructed on a basis of efficient agriculture. In Chile,
government and landowners alike treat the land with contempt.
Agricultural population has fallen by a third since 1939. Agricultural output is growing by only 1.6 percent annually, while
population increases by nearly 2 percent and per capita food
consumption by 2.3 percent. As a result, Chile, potentially one
of the world's richest agricultural areas, with more than a hectare
of cultivable land per capita, has become a net importer of food,
the cost of which now constitutes a quarter of her import bill.

Why this astonishing anomaly? Because the Chilean social
structure virtually prohibits efficient agriculture. Some 86 percent of the agricultural area is divided into large *fundos,* whose
owners find it more profitable to speculate in land than to
farm it, still less to invest in it. Alongside them are the even
more backward *minifundia,* whose wretched tenants cannot produce enough to feed themselves, let alone purchase a modest
entry into the modern consumer civilization. Between these two
groups, every refinement of bad farming is practised—vertical
ploughing of sloping land, the fallow system, burning of forests
and bush. Only a few miles from Santiago I examined estates
whose composition and techniques have scarcely changed since
the 17th century—giant colonial houses, with clusters of mud
*peon* huts grouped carefully out of smelling distance at the
gateway, vast tracts of rich, weed-covered land, an aroma of
arrogant decay. The government naturally refuses to dispossess
the landowners whom it represents; in any case, abrupt change
would offend the iron laws of the Washington bankers. When

the recent earthquake, which devastated the south, offered a unique chance for peaceful structural reform—to be financed with the aid which flowed to Chile from all over the world— the government allowed the relief administration to drift into the hands of local dignitaries, mainly big landowners, who have thus been able to buttress their economic position. The peasants got bowls of soup and the odd blanket. A Chilean economist said to me: "Our earthquakes are nature's revenge on us for the way we treat its riches." Meanwhile, back in Washington, the bankers wonder why things don't seem to get any better, and resignedly blame it all on the Latin American temperament.

Despite their immense differences, Peru is imprisoned in the same vicious circle as Chile. Here again, the U.S. banker is the real arbiter (the government even went so far as to engage a U.S. business-efficiency firm to tell it how to run the country), bestowing periodic loans—such as $200 million for the vast Toquelala copper project—in return for financial and political orthodoxy. Peru has been in the clutches of the bankers longer than most; as a result, it has more convenient laws for foreign companies and imports than almost anywhere else. In Lima, at the delightful Bolivar Hotel (where colonial service and comfort survive), I got Cooper's Oxford Marmalade for breakfast, and could stroll around the amply stocked store of Sears-Roebuck (Peru) Inc. Nearby, workmen were erecting a 90-foot Cinerama screen, believed to be the biggest in the world. Across the river was the other side of the story: the diseased warrens of slums; and, once outside the tiny coastal plain, the desolate misery of a man-made lunar landscape.

Peru has some of the richest and most diverse mineral deposits in the world. But three quarters of its inhabitants are virtually outside the money economy, most of them subsisting on the borderline of starvation. There are very few roads. The most important railway, from Lima to Huancayo, is a mere 260 miles, and has two trains a day each way. The richest part of the country—east of the Andes—is almost uninhabited; to get from its centre, Iquitos, to Lima, goods must be transported via the Amazon and the Panama Canal. The Indians on the high Andean plateau, the old heart of the Inca emprire, cohabit with their white and *mestizo* masters in silent, passive hostility, eating a low-calory diet of corn and potatoes and, on every possible occasion, getting drunk on a mixture of *chicha* (fermented corn), raw spirit, and urine. Here, as elsewhere in the Andes, the mood is introspective, sullen with despair: the Andean cities have the highest (though statistically unrecorded) suicide rates in the world. Where progress has penetrated—in the shape of mining—it has brought with it only concrete hutments for the workers and a ubiquitous veneer of evil gray slime, which smells like death. The Andean mining towns are the most horrific examples of human degradation I have ever seen.

Yet Peru is, nominally, a democracy; in the Apra, it has one of the oldest and most powerful left-wing political movements in the continent. In Lima, Apra headquarters—which nightly supply free dentistry and medical treatment, free drugs, subsidized meals, and classes from basic arithmetic to painting in oils—are a thriving center of purposeful socialist activity. But between the Apra and real power a great gulf is fixed. One of its leaders told me frankly: "If we were elected to power, democratically, and attempted to carry through structural reforms, the army would instantly suspend the constitution and reimpose dictatorship. Instead, at this stage, we must be content to ensure that the democratic forms are observed and work through the conservatives."

Here we touch on one of the basic problems of Latin America. Democracy is largely a facade: even where its ceremonies are tolerated, the army is the ultimate arbiter. In Peru, the Left dare not assume power, for fear that it would lose even its formal privileges. Elsewhere, where the Left has won elections, the fruits of office have turned into bitter ashes. We have already seen, in Argentina, a so-called extreme left government operating a police tyranny to pursue a policy of deflation dictated by foreign bankers. Much the same could be said of Venezuela, where the triumphant electoral victory of President Betancourt's left-wing Accion Democratica has been followed by social stagnation and heartbreaking disillusion.

Indeed, in all the centuries of economic madness which have been Latin America's bitter lot, the story of postwar Venezuela is outstanding for sheer, stark lunacy. Since the war, this country has become the world's largest exporter and second

largest producer of oil, and it has managed to secure a bigger
cut of the royalties than any other country except the U.S.
itself. Under the crackpot Jimenez régime—which received
Washington's benevolent accolade for economic "realism"—
something like £1,000 million were thrown to the winds on a
spending spree which makes the Sheik of Kuwait look like a
mere treble-chance winner. A vast hydro-electric power station
was built, before anyone ascertained whether there would
be any demand for it (there wasn't). A steel works was purchased—without any coke ovens, and without providing a coke
supply. Near Caracas, jungle mountains were levelled for building lots for Jimenez and his cronies: their palatial villas now
stand, incomplete and desolate, like Ozymandias' trunk.

Jimenez's most characteristic folly was the Humboldt Hotel,
built on the top of a 7,000-foot mountain overlooking Caracas.
This is undoubtedly the most magnificent hotel I have ever
been privileged to enter. Unfortunately it can only be reached
by a terrifying cable railway, and for a lot of the time its superb
views over the city and the Caribbean are obscured in impenetr-
able, icy cloud. Its sheer, 14 storeys make it look like a desolate
lighthouse in thick fog, and only the odd visitor with a morbid
obsession for heights and mist cares to stay there. Naturally, it is
run (by the state) at an enormous loss.

Betancourt, as the first constitutionally elected president
of modern times, inherited the consequences of this profligacy:
the highest-cost economy in the world, which is driving Venezuelan oil out of world markets; seven different police forces; a
huge, overpaid bureaucracy; inflated armed forces equipped
with expensive gadgets like supersonic fighters (he has recently
had to placate them by ordering, of all things, a nuclear sub-
marine); and a great sheaf of unpaid bills. Naturally, he stopped
work on some of Jimenez's more ludicrous projects, thus immediately swelling Caracas' ugly mob of unemployed, and putting his government in pawn to the army. The collapse of world
oil prices has meanwhile knocked the bottom out of the Venezuelan oil boom; new exploration is not merely failing to keep
pace with current production, but the two largest oil companies
are, for the first time since oil was discovered there, shipping
exploration equipment from Venezuela to other theaters. In-

evitably, Betancourt, too, was forced to turn to the U.S. for loans, with all that this entails in social and economic stagnation. Basic land reform has been shelved, a credit squeeze imposed, and unemployment is swelling. The growing anger of the mob can be balanced only by more concessions to the army. The Left is split into warring factions. When I arrived in Caracas, tanks were in the streets, violence in the muggy air. It cost me 10 shillings to buy a glass of milk and from my hotel bedroom (well above Savoy prices, but crawling with cockroaches nevertheless) I could see human bundles of rags littering the streets. And Caracas is the El Dorado of the richest country in Latin America.

And so to Cuba. The outlines of Castro's remarkable revolution I have already described in an earlier article. Here, all I need do is to recall its salient characteristics. First, Castro came to power, like Mao Tse-tung, through a peasant revolution which completely obliterated the traditional military establishment in the process. Secondly, he governs through a genuine dictatorship of the proletariat: his rule is arbitrary, its sole— but vital—mandate being the overwhelming support of the majority. Thirdly, he has destroyed the basis of capitalist (chiefly foreign) economic power by seizing, without compensation, all its major units, including the landed estates. Fourthly, he has buttressed his ability to withstand economic pressure by agreements with the Communist bloc.

This combination of factors makes the Cuban experiment unique in Latin American history. Will the other Latin American republics be obliged to imitate it? It looks increasingly likely. In my view, barring some fundamental change in United States policy, social democracy—the acquisition of power by constitutionally elected parties of the Left—cannot provide an early and effective solution to the really critical problems of the area. In certain states—Costa Rica and Uruguay are two obvious examples—gradualist methods have been applied with real, if limited, success. But both these countries happily possess highly literate and homogeneous populations, almost exclusively of European origin; their economic problems are open to clearcut solutions whch can be intelligibly explained to educated electorates. As such, they are exceptional.

For most of Latin America, the choice is more stark. No attempt to solve its basic economic problems can be made without fundamental changes in the social structure. At present, these cannot be brought about through mere electoral victories, since effective legislation requires the assent of the armed forces. Until these vested interests are destroyed—as they were in Cuba —the democratic process remains a farce. Latin America, therefore, does not really possess the alternative of reformism; its only way to progress is through a genuine revolution, involving the dispossession by confiscation of the propertied classes and their ally, foreign capital. Such a revolution may come about under the influence of *Fidelismo*; but if it is sufficiently delayed, the entire initiative of change may be thrown into the welcoming hands of the Communists—under the direction not even of accommodating Russia, but of intransigent China.

# THE COMING LATIN AMERICAN REVOLUTION

## BY A TRAVELING OBSERVER

What are the reasons for expecting a massive upheaval in Latin America in coming years, probably sooner rather than later?

It would be indeed strange if this large part of the world were to escape the social convulsions that have rocked most areas of the planet since the beginning of this century. As a matter of fact, it was the Mexican Revolution of 1910 that historically set off the present cycle of world change; and the conditions that produced it can be found, in varying degree, in all the countries of Latin America, not even excluding Uruguay whose peaceful revolution of 1911 created a stability of sorts that has endured, and not even excluding Mexico itself. The case of Cuba is well known—here a genuine revolution whose future is still in doubt changed existing patterns of land and capital ownership. Bolivia has a revolutionary government, but it also has the lowest per capita income on the continent and conditions of dire poverty make further upheavals almost certain. The other 16 nations, without exception, can be said to stand in the shadow of revolution; some are very close to it, particularly Brazil, where a genuine overturn on the Cuban model would probably take on continental proportions.

No observer of Latin American affairs, from inside or outside, interested or disinterested, expert or otherwise, sees any easy way out of Latin America's growing economic stagnation. The problems are too great, the needed changes too fundamental, the mounting difficulties of the entire region too grave and formidable for facile solution.

Consider the problem of population and food. It is a commonplace to say that Latin America is hungry. On a per capita basis, the area actually produces and eats less food than

---

The author of this article is a United States businessman whose job requires him to travel often and widely throughout Latin America.

it did before World War II. Today the population stands at 200 million. In countries like Venezuela, the population doubles in 18 years, outstripping all efforts at land reform, and creating a growing problem of feeding the hungry. During the next 40 years, the population of Latin America is expected to grow to 600 million, giving the United States real minority status in the Hemisphere. Is it possible for anyone to suggest a reasonable method of feeding such enormous masses of people, masses that will be landless and unemployed in far greater proportions than today when most major cities are already surrounded by festering slums of the hungry and the desperate?

In Brazil, approximately 5 percent of the population owns nearly 95 percent of the land; in Venezuela, 2 percent owns 74 percent; in Ecuador, one-third of the land belongs to less than one-fifth of 1 percent of the people. For the entire area, less than 5 percent of the landowners own roughly 70 percent of all the arable land. Outside of Cuba, there has never been a genuine land reform in Latin America. Even the Mexican program has been a failure. Is there any reason to believe that the owners of these lands will give them to the landless? And if they were willing, under some form of compensation, would there be time for such reforms? The evidence seems to indicate a negative answer. In Mexico, lands that have been distributed are finding their way back into the hands of large owners through foreclosures by the banks.* Venezuela's relatively ambitious program of land distribution by democratic means seems to lag far behind population increase; and, again outside of Cuba, this is the brightest spot in the land reform picture in all Latin America.

The governing classes in Latin America are among the most backward, self-centered, and conservative in the world. If they fear for the stability of their country, they send their money abroad. Most of them send much of it abroad anyway, just to be safe. They care little or nothing about the welfare

---

* Even where this has not happened, the defenseless small landowner has found himself increasingly oppressed and exploited by a growing tribe of usurers, middlemen, dealers, etc. The Mexican experience proves decisively that fragmentation of estates into small landholdings is no solution of the problem.—Ed.

of the people. They even steal the food and other aid sent in as earthquake and disaster relief. The food is fed to their cattle. This shows how much they really care about human welfare. It is quite useless to ask them to divide their lands for motives of altruism, and they too cannot fail to see that the United States has made the chief aim of its Latin American policy the overthrow of the one government—Cuba—that has carried out a sweeping land reform program.

For many reasons, capital flows out of Latin America faster than it comes in. Fluctuations in market prices of basic commodities such as coffee, sugar, copper, tin, lead, and oil on which the economies of whole countries depend take away much, leave little, and the trend is steadily against Latin America. Foreign ownership draws out capital: foreign shareholders want their profits. Attacks on this practice, as in Brazil at present, frighten foreign investors, and desperately needed capital stays away. The Cuban expropriations and fear of similar happenings elsewhere accelerate the trend. Meanwhile, many of those with wealth continue to send it abroad, or at best to invest it in unproductive land which pays a much lower tax than industrial enterprise. Inflation plagues the entire region. In Brazil, the purchasing power of the cruzeiro has been cut in half in a year. In Venezuela, the bolívar, though fixed at approximately four to the U.S. dollar, buys about half of what 25¢ would buy in the United States. Chile's cost of living is near the top in Latin America. The struggle to get by becomes harder all the time for wage earners. Per capita annual income in Latin America averages from less than $100 to around $700 at the peak, and the reality is even worse because of the disproportionately large incomes of those at the top. It is very common in the whole region for many to live without money and with little food, clothing, or shelter. In the environs of Santiago de Chile and other large cities are colonies of people living at an almost animal level.

One traveling in Latin America today, particularly in every part of the South American continent, experiences a strange feeling of impending change. It is the sort of feeling that one would probably have had traveling in Russia before 1917, in France before 1789—the feeling that change, of epochal proportions, is in the making; that one of the great dramas of human history is about to take place. There is the expectation, expressed often in the words of sober businessmen, that things cannot go on as they are. There are the constant roundups of leftists which turn the prisons into modern counterparts of the French Bastille. This is true even in Mexico, most stable of the Latin American republics, where David Alfaro Siqueiros, a painter of world fame, is among those imprisoned on charges of "social dissolution." It is in the constant changes of government, and threats of change, sweeping through the area; witness Brazil, Ecuador, and the Dominican Republic in recent months. It is true that governmental instability has always been a fact of life in Latin America; but the overturns of today obey deeper historical laws, and there is always profound mass unrest at the base. It is in the day's news—the growth of armed robbery on the streets, the steady deterioration of municipal utilities, the growing banditry in the rural areas.

When businessmen, working in off hours in the slums surrounding Lima in an effort to improve conditions for the wretched beings who live there, say that they expect the mobs to invade Lima next year or the year after that, maybe they do not really mean it, but enough of them say it to show that the fear is there. This is not a condition found only in Lima; it can be found, and the same expressions of fear and concern can be heard, in most major South American cities—Santiago, Rio de Janeiro, Caracas, Guayaquil. Labor, though often weak and poorly led, keeps the area in turmoil through constant strikes and street demonstrations often ending in violence—general strikes called at will and thoroughly enforced, multiple strikes tying up several branches of industry at the same time, single-industry strikes. The authorities can't or won't do much about these strikes and demonstrations; they are generally tolerated as in the nature of things, as perhaps a way of letting the masses blow off steam without getting entirely out of hand. These do not appear to be the manifestations of the growing pains of industrialism, though there is an element of this too; rather they seem to be the symptoms of grave social disease, with the dispossessed and vengeful millions swarming at the vortex of every disorder. What can be expected in the years ahead as these starving multitudes multiply to catastrophic proportions in all the cities where even now they represent an unmanageable problem?

One does not have to go to leftist sources to discover sympathy with social change in the leading countries of Latin America. It is in fact surprising to find so many businessmen, engineers, and industrial technicians who are in agreement that things can't keep on as they are much longer. This opinion, coming from an engineer in Argentina who has no sympathy for Communism, is typical of many: "The system of free enterprise is on trial; if it is not able to provide the jobs, build the plants, feed the people, give them houses, then another system will be tried. People now know that they do not have to put up with unbearable conditions. They know about the progress being made in countries like Russia and China through systems of public ownership; and if they decide that the present system offers no way out for them, they will try the new methods."

This is an expression of a growing feeling one finds throughout the world, particularly among thinking people who are not Communists and are even active opponents of the Communist doctrine, that systems of public ownership are forming a new society that is already stronger than that of the West and that will give the world its predominant complexion for years to come. This feeling is especially widespread among intellectual circles in Latin America where there is much speculation on the subject, particularly Latin America's place in the world of the future. The opinion of the young engineer quoted above is a fairly common one. The constant uproar in the universities carries strong overtones along these lines. It is felt that the new society, centered in Russia, Asia, and Africa, now offers a real alternative to the traditional system of the West.

Governor Luis Muñoz Marin of Puerto Rico said recently that it is not a question of whether or not there will be revolution in Latin America, it is a question of who will be in charge of it, democratic forces or totalitarian forces.

What are the real chances for the democratic approach? It is by no means certain that the Alliance for Progress program, even if effectively applied, could do very much to alter the course of events in Latin America. The drift toward fundamental change, part of one of the great movements of world history, moves forward, with the continent in its glacial grip. But it is not certain either that the Alliance for Progress can be brought into effective being. Dr. Milton Eisenhower has said: "Our dilemma, as I see it, is that we cannot possibly afford not to meet commitments to Latin America, but neither can we seemingly afford to finance them." Secretary of the Treasury Douglas Dillon has said the United States "will be a partner in hemispheric progress, but we do not intend, and in fact we cannot, carry the whole load." Land and tax reforms would be necessary for U.S. aid to be effective, and these reforms are not coming into being at a rate that gives the Alliance for Progress any real chance of success. A further grave obstacle to the success of the Alliance is that aid may be tied to anti-Castro action—this may be one lasting result of the most recent Punta del Este conference—and if this is the case, then the Alliance for Progress seems doomed throughout most of Latin America, leaving it to operate only in peripheral areas around the Caribbean.

What will happen then in Latin America? What one can expect is strong movements in two directions—toward upheavals seeking social change in a radical way, as in Cuba; and toward military regimes striving to head off social change through repression. But military power may be totally ineffective when the time comes—for the long pull, this is certain to be so. The whole weakness of the Latin American situation is that, in the long view, there is no viable status quo to maintain.

A real overturn in a big country like Brazil, which will have close to 100 million population by 1970, could throw all of South America into the throes of revolution. Brazil is in dire straits; financial collapse dogs its heels; its potential Castros are already active; lands are being seized by the landless in many areas. The military may step in the next time around, but with conditions rapidly growing worse, as they are, genuine revolution might find the military divided against itself. The result could be a dictatorship of the Left, as in Cuba. This would tip the scales for all Latin America.

The chances are more than two to one that this will be the outcome, and soon. It is later than most of us think—far later—

in all of Latin America. History has not planned to leave this vast continent out of the great tides of change sweeping the earth. It seems only that Latin America was destined to close a historic cycle, as it began it, by staging its revolution last.

# WHICH WAY FOR LATIN AMERICA?

## BY LEO HUBERMAN

Two thirds of the people of the world are permanently hungry.

Among the hungriest are the people of Latin America. Their poverty is shown by the income figures. In 1953, when Fidel Castro first took up arms against Batista, average annual per capita income for Mississippi, the poorest state in the United States, was $829. For most of the Latin American countries, it was under $300, or less than 40 percent of Mississippi's.

A per capita income of less than $300 a year marks a country as "underdeveloped." What is an underdeveloped country like? The best short answer to that question that I have seen comes from the excellent pamphlet, *One Hundred Countries, One and One Quarter Billion People,* by Paul Hoffman, published in 1960 by the Committee for International Economic Growth, Washington, D.C.:

> Everyone knows an underdeveloped country when he sees one. It is a country characterized by poverty, with beggars in the cities, and villages eking out a bare subsistence in the rural areas. It is a country lacking in factories of its own, usually with inadequate supplies of power and light. It usually has insufficient roads and railroads, insufficient government services, poor communications. It has few hospitals, and few institutions of higher learning. Most of its people cannot read or write. In spite of the generally prevailing poverty of the people, it may have isolated islands of wealth, with a few persons living in luxury. Its banking system is poor; small loans have to be obtained through money lenders who are often little better than extortionists. Another striking characteristic of an underdeveloped country is that its exports to other countries usually consist almost entirely of raw materials, ores, or fruits, or some staple product with possibly a small admixture of luxury handicrafts. Often the extraction or cultivation of these raw material exports is in the hands of foreign companies.

*This is the text of a talk given to the Swarthmore College International Club, December 16, 1960.*

This description fits most of the Latin American countries like a glove. Take the last part—"its exports to other countries usually consist almost entirely of raw materials, ores, or fruits"— and consider a few figures for the proportion of total exports: Chile—copper 71 percent; Bolivia—tin 58 percent; Brazil—coffee 62 percent; Honduras—bananas 57 percent; Cuba—sugar 79 percent; Venezuela—oil 92 percent. These figures show how much the economies of the Latin American countries are in imbalance—so distorted that though they are predominantly agricultural countries, yet they must import large quantities of the food they eat.

Are these poverty-stricken nations poor because they lack natural resources? Not at all. They have an abundance of the resources necessary to make a country rich. No continent in the world compares with Latin America in the amount of cultivable, high-yield soil, or in reserves of timber. List the metals important to industrial development—copper, tin, iron, silver, gold, zinc, lead—all of them and many others, as well as oil, are found in great abundance in Latin America.

And so it is with many of the other underdeveloped countries of the world. They too are rich in natural resources—yet the masses of their people remain hungry, unemployed, poorly clothed, badly housed, illiterate, disease-ridden. This has been their lot for many years, but today something new has been added. Where formerly the hungry of the earth accepted their lot as the decree of fate, now they no longer do so. They have learned that hunger, illiteracy, disease, need not be the "natural order" of things. They know now that there is a way out. They want to change their status from that of an underdeveloped country to that of a developed country—and they want to do it *fast*.

What is the best way to bring about that change as rapidly as possible? Can it best be done via capitalism or socialism?

To find the answer to that question we must first ask, what are the forces that promote economic development? What is there about the rich countries of the world that marks them off from the poor countries? Compare the underdeveloped country of India with the highly developed country, the United States. What does the United States have that India lacks? One thing, for example, is steel. The per capita production of steel in India in 1955-1956 was less than 7 lbs.; in the United States it was 1300 lbs. At the same time, India had three times more reserves of iron ore than the United States. From iron ore steel is made. But in 1955-1956, the United States had roughly 200 times more steel per person than India had. And because it had more steel, it had more and better tools and machinery with which it made more goods which gave it a higher standard of living.

The lesson is plain. It is not enough to have a wealth of natural resources—they must be used effectively. That means they must be worked on and processed, not in the older slower ways, but with the newer, more efficient, more scientific techniques that go with the use of machinery. An underdeveloped country is one which has fallen behind technologically. The answer for India—and it is the same for all the underdeveloped countries—is to increase the stock of tools and machinery, to transform the processes of production through the application of modern technology. In short the answer is, to industrialize.

How can this be done? So long as man produced just enough to feed and clothe himself—but no more—then the possibility of economic development did not exist. But when man learned to produce more than was required for his own sustenance, that additional amount, the surplus above his needs, could be accumulated and invested in such a way as to make the community progressively richer.*

Everything depends on what is done with the margin above the subsistence needs of society, the difference between what a country produces and what it consumes—the economic surplus. From the point of view of economic development, of industrializing a country, there is a right way and a wrong way to use the economic surplus. If it is siphoned off by the wealthy and powerful and spent on luxurious living, as King Saud does with the hundreds of millions of dollars he receives in oil royalties; or if it is appropriated by an imperialist power, as the United States did in Cuba; or if it is hoarded, or spent on jewelry and trinkets; or if it is wasted on the upkeep of a corrupt government, or (the

---

* The best analysis of the problem of underdeveloped countries—a real contribution to the subject—is *The Political Economy of Growth* by Paul A. Baran, Monthly Review Press, 1957.

typical Latin-American way) on the maintenance of a military establishment designed to preserve the status quo, then there will be no real economic development.

But if the economic surplus is properly mobilized and directed, if it is invested in new skills, in factories and railways and machines to make machines, that is, if it is invested in the means of production, then there will be economic development. Where the economic surplus was so utilized, as in the countries of northwestern Europe during the past few centuries, there modern industry was created and the countries became rich.

In these capitalist countries in the period of the Industrial Revolution and after, the process went along these lines: to their domestically produced economic surplus were added fabulous amounts of gold, silver, and treasures accumulated through the conquest and plunder of countries in North and South America, Africa, and Asia. The labor force needed for the factories came from peasants pushed off the land and handicraftsmen unable to compete with the new machine-made goods. The workers, often including women and very young children, were paid miserably low wages—just enough to keep them alive in unsanitary, overcrowded slum hovels. Working conditions in the badly-ventilated, poorly-lighted factories were inhuman. Profits to the employers, the industrial bourgeoisie, were high; these profits were saved then plowed back into the business; to this capital was added further continued plunder from other lands as well as borrowed capital from abroad.

The industrial bourgeoisie met with the opposition of the feudal lords whose way of life was being disrupted. It overcame this opposition and became the dominant class in society. Thus it was in a position to control the state and use the state machinery for the continued exploitation of the peasants and workers and to advance its own interests. Karl Marx, describing the process, said of the industrial bourgeoisie: "They all employ the power of the State, the concentrated and organized force of society, to hasten, hothouse fashion, the transformation of the feudal mode of production into the capitalist mode, and to shorten the transition." (*Capital,* Kerr ed., Vol. I, p. 823.)

Production was increased, the profits were again saved and reinvested, and newer and better and bigger machines were in-

vented and put into operation. At the same time the technical
advances comparable to those made in manufacturing were made
in agriculture also, so that over the years, fewer and fewer people
on the land were turning out more and more farm products to
feed the swelling population working in industry in the cities. In
this process of industrial development the countries were themselves transformed; such far-reaching changes in the way production was organized and carried on brought inevitable changes in
the lives of the people.

This is an oversimplified, thumbnail sketch of the industrial
development process in the capitalist countries of northwestern
Europe. There were variations in the different countries, of
course, but this was roughly the pattern. Industrial development
in the United States was markedly different in several respects
but here too the basic pattern of accumulated capital and productivity—of large profits, large savings, investment, increased
production, reinvestment of savings—was the same. And, to the
surprise of many of you, I am sure, the role of the State in this
country was also of tremendous importance just as it had been
in Europe. Professor E. S. Mason, in his *Promoting Economic
Development* (1955) says on this subject:

Most Americans are unaware of the extent to which the
Federal and State governments promoted the early economic development of the United States through the provision of social
capital in the form of canals, river development, turnpikes, railway
facilities, and the like. The provision of public works of this sort by
government was, of course, essential to the expansion of private
investment.

These were the methods, then, whereby capital was accumulated and industry built up in the developed capitalist countries over hundreds of years.

This basic pattern for capitalist economic development,
modified to suit the special conditions prevailing in the first
socialist country in the world, brought the desired result there,
too. When the Bolsheviks seized power in Russia in 1917, their
country was way behind the United States and the advanced
countries of northwest Europe. The Communists wanted to catch
up—fast. They felt the necessity of getting rich quick and they

were determined to take all the steps necessary for economic development—no matter how great the cost.

Where industrialization was a happen-so in the capitalist countries, with individual profit-seeking entrepreneurs as the driving force, in the socialist USSR where the economic surplus was socially controlled, it was a planned effort, with the government as the sole owner of the means of production deciding just how the economic surplus was to be invested to achieve the desired goal.

The Soviet planners were faced with a difficult choice. The people were ill-fed, ill-clothed, and ill-housed. Investment in consumers' goods plant would furnish more to eat, more clothes to wear, more houses to live in right away; investment in production for consumption would mean more immediate well-being, more of the necessary things of life now. *But* (and it was an important but) if this policy were to be followed, there would be little more in the distant future than in the next few years.

On the other hand, if whatever capital investment was available from taxation and savings and exports were poured into building factories, machinery, power dams, and railways, then there would be less to eat, drink, and wear now, but there would be much more later. Investment in the means of production for capital goods meant sacrifices now—but well-being in the future.

The Soviet Union chose the second path and poured all available resources into expanding the country's productive plant. Coming late on the industrialization scene it had the advantage —as have all the underdeveloped countries—of immediately adopting the latest, most improved techniques of production that the earlier industrialized nations had perfected after centuries of development. It could skip the intermediate stages of technical evolution and start with the most advanced methods. But in all other respects it had to start from scratch. Practically every other advanced country in the world, the United States included, had been helped on the road to industrialization by foreign capital which enabled it to buy the machinery and other supplies it needed while it was beginning to put up its own factories. For the Communists, for a long time, there was no such help, and when it did come the terms were outrageously onerous.

But in spite of the many hardships, the people of the Soviet

Union continued their forced march toward industrialization. There was always an acute shortage of consumption goods, the population was squeezed in a hundred different ways so the economic surplus could be made larger and invested and reinvested in heavy industry; the sacrifices and suffering were tremendous—forced labor, imposed collectivization of agriculture at breakneck speed, an omnipotent secret police with its inevitable accompaniment of false arrests, imprisonment, executions.

At the same time, an advanced health and social security program was instituted, an illiterate nation was educated in schools which are today the envy of the most advanced nations of the capitalist world. The caliber of Soviet education and the quality of its industrial skill and technological know-how were demonstrated in an unforgettably dramatic fashion with the launching of Sputniks I and II in the fall of 1957. After that remarkable achievement, Soviet statistics of incomparably rapid industrial growth could no longer be dismissed as mere propaganda; no longer could there be any doubt that the Soviet goal of economic development had been achieved in the record time of 40 years. The USSR had done in four decades what capitalist countries had taken three centuries to accomplish. Today the Soviet Union is one of the world's greatest industrialized nations; it is in a position, at long last, to begin to furnish its people with the consumption goods and everything else that makes for a high standard of living that they have for so long been without.

Which way for Latin America? Will it be the capitalist way, or the socialist way? Will it be the capitalist system with private ownership of the means of production, based on the premise that the self-interest of the business man is sure to benefit the nation; that if only individuals are left free to make as much profit as they can, the whole of society must be better off; that the best way to get things done is to let capitalists make as much profit as possible out of doing them; and that, as an inevitable by-product of the process, the needs of the people will be served?

Or will it be the socialist system with public ownership of the means of production and centralized planning, based on a revolutionary change involving the reconstruction of society along entirely different lines: instead of individual effort for individual profit—collective effort for collective benefit; instead of anarchic production for profit—planned production for use, insuring jobs for all, all the time, with economic security from the cradle to the grave?

My own answer is that the Latin American countries—and all other underdeveloped countries—cannot take the steps necessary for economic development unless they choose the socialist way. Political independence, though of the utmost importance, is not enough; they must win economic independence too. And economic independence in the sense of establishing their own control over their own economic surplus so they can apply it to productive capital investment for the planned economic development of the whole nation, involves those far-reaching social changes which spell revolution and socialism.

Cuba is showing the way. In the *New York Times Magazine* of Sunday, December 4, 1960, Senator Mike Mansfield addressed himself to "The Basic Problem of Latin America." Here is what he proposes must be done by any Latin American nation that wishes to develop:

(1) It must act, at once, to alleviate the most glaring inadequacies in diet, housing and health from which tens of millions of people suffer.

(2) It must improve agriculture by diversifying crops, broadening land ownership, expanding cultivable acreage and introducing modern agricultural techniques on a wide scale in order to increase production, particularly of food.

(3) It must bring about the establishment of a steadily expanding range of industries.

(4) It must wipe out illiteracy within a few years and provide adequate facilities to educate an ever-increasing number of highly trained technicians, specialists and professionals to provide the whole range of modern services.

(5) It must end the relative isolation of the beachheads from the interiors and the parts of the interior from one another by a vast enlargement of existing systems of transportation and communications.

Now the interesting thing about this excellent prescription for curing the ills of the Latin American countries is that it is an age-old remedy prescribed by equally competent doctors years and years ago. In different words which said the same thing, it was prescribed for Cuba by the Foreign Policy Association in 1935, by the World Bank in 1950, and by the United States Department of Commerce in 1956; but the medicine was never swallowed—until the revolutionary government of Cuba came to power. Now, at long last, the things that needed doing, the measures for making Cuba a healthy instead of a sick nation, have been taken. What Senator Mansfield and the Foreign Policy Association and the World Bank and the Department of Commerce said had to be done *is* being done—in *socialist* Cuba. But it is not being done in any of the capitalist-feudal, colonial countries of Latin America. Nor, I am suggesting, can it be done in those countries unless and until they too have their own socialist revolutions.

This is the lesson to be learned from the Cuban Revolution —a vitally important lesson for all Latin American countries. The experience of Cuba proves beyond a doubt that a social revolution is an indispensable precondition for the initiation of economic growth and social development.

Cuba, before the Revolution, demonstrated the extent of mismanagement, inefficiency, waste, and exploitation imposed upon an underdeveloped country by monopoly capitalism. The mere removal of the imperialist yoke enabled revolutionary Cuba to put into immediate cultivation vast areas of fertile land previously neglected or misused by absentee landowners, to put to immediate use industrial capacity previously kept idle. The adoption of a centrally planned economy is enabling Cuba to go further, to lay the groundwork of a balanced, healthy, cultured, and eventually rich society.

That is the lesson of Cuba for underdeveloped countries— that without a social revolution there is no possibility of going beyond the introduction of largely ineffectual reforms. The experience of the Soviet Union and of China proved it before; now Cuba has proved it again. The Latin American countries may not have learned the lesson from distant Russia and China, but it will be driven home to them by the example of neighboring Cuba.

# THE VARIETIES OF LAND REFORM

## BY ANDREW GUNDER FRANK

Land reform projects are mushrooming all over the globe. But not all land reform programs are the same. In Latin America, especially under the impetus of the Alliance for Progress, several countries have passed or are discussing land reform laws. Concerned and progressive people everywhere scrutinize these proposals and laws, and often criticize them for being too mild or otherwise misdirected. It is important to distinguish between the varieties of land reform proposals and counter-proposals and to learn which deserve support and which opposition.

Fundamental to any analysis of the problem of land reform is the fact that it is not so much an administrative, or even an economic, as it is an essentially political, process. Beginning, then, with this notion of a political process, we can conveniently distinguish three types of supposed land reform.

The first excludes any significant political change. It is the type of "land reform" proposed by conservatives. It is exemplified by the laws which the legislatures, often controlled by the landowners themselves, have recently found it convenient or necessary to pass in several Latin American countries today. In the same category should be included the voluntary donations of land by the Church or by the landowners themselves. This type of land reform is the last resort of the landowner and is really no reform at all.

The second attempts to incorporate all or part of the peasantry into the already existing national political community. This type of land reform finds much support among the critics of the first type and is proposed by several political groups, among them in Latin America the Christian Democrats and, more often than not, the Communists. It has been exemplified

The author taught economics for four years at Michigan State University. During the last year he has been in Latin America studying conditions in the various countries at first hand.

in the Mexico of Cárdenas, the Guatemala of Arbenz, the Egypt of Nasser. My contention will be that, however persuasive the arguments in favor of it, land reform which aims merely to integrate the peasantry into the existing social order is likely to fail even to meet the announced ends of its proponents.

The third attempts from the outset to effect a rapid and fundamental transformation of the existing order itself. It begins with a far-reaching change in the entire society, as exemplified in Cuba, and appears to be the only type which can meet minimum demands. It is therefore the only type of land reform worthy of the name.

A convenient index—although, as we shall see, it is also more than that—by which to distinguish the various types of land reform is the speed, or lack of speed, with which the reform is undertaken. At the rate at which land was distributed in Guatemala in the post-Arbenz years (1955 to 1961), it would take 148 years for all peasant families to receive some land—if there were no population growth in the meantime. The return to United Fruit and other owners, of land previously expropriated, the purchase by the government of worn-out lands, and other related measures indicate that the Guatemala "reform" falls into the first type, in which there is no political change whatever. In Venezuela, the government of which is often cited as making a real effort at a land reform in depth, the Presidential propaganda figures speak of 50 thousand families receiving 3.5 million acres of land in the nearly 4 years of the Betancourt government. (See, for example, *Time* magazine, March 1, 1963, p. 22.) However, in a report recently published jointly by the Venezuelan National Agrarian Institute, the Ministry of Agriculture, the Agrarian Bank, and the National Planning Office, it appears that in the last 25 years, all put together, no more than 1.4 million acres have been distributed to 35,622 families. It is not specified how much of this was distributed during the tenure of the present government. *On the other hand, it is true that 3.5 million acres were expropriated and paid for, often at exorbitant prices and in cash amounts in excess of the maximum prescribed by law.* This particular "land reform," in other words, has been big business for the landowners who have been able to sell no-longer-wanted land, and no doubt, to invest the proceeds elsewhere (including abroad). The land reform laws recently enacted in Peru and Chile are even milder than the reforms already put into practice in Guatemala and Venezuela. Almost all imaginable protection is afforded to the landowner rather than to the peasant. The conclusion is inescapable: measures of this type are not land reforms at all. They are out and out frauds.

The second type of land reform merits more serious discussion. Its advocates propose to incorporate the peasants into the social and political life of the nation through a process which mobilizes all of the progressive forces against the conservatives but which leaves the foundations of their power intact. The reformers would seek at the same time to redirect rural credit, technical assistance, etc., so that these measures would benefit the peasants and not just the medium and large landowners, as at present. The time period envisaged is usually of the order of 5 to 15 years. Variations on this second type of land reform can be found in the experience of Mexico, of Guatemala before the counter-revolution of 1954, and of Egypt since 1952.

It seems to this writer that the viability of this second type of land reform is highly questionable, both on theoretical grounds and on the evidence of historical experience. Two dangers, especially, arise which threaten its success: The first is that leaving the power of the conservatives intact ensures continued opposition to the reforms and puts roadblocks in the way of mobilizing the progressive forces. Though they may have been pushed out of governmental office, the conservatives nevertheless retain the ability to slow down and ultimately destroy the land reform. They can refuse to provide necessary investment funds, they can sabotage the operation of government agencies charged with implementing the reforms, organize hostile propaganda campaigns, enlist foreign support against their own government, and so on. At the same time, the political jockeying and maneuvering that progressives must engage in to counter this conservative opposition, demands compromises which tend to undermine the reform and turn it into a series of half measures.

The second danger is that carrying out a land reform at

the slow rate of 5 to 15 years and within the framework of the
existing institutions creates groups which acquire a vested interest in maintaining their new advantages and which therefore
readily ally themselves with conservatives in opposing the extension of the same benefits to still other groups.

The relevance and importance of these obstacles are demonstrated by the attempts, both successful and unsuccessful, to
complete a land reform of the second type. The 1952 land
reform of the Arbenz government in Guatemala was, of course,
much swifter and more far-reaching than the so-called reforms
of recent years in that country. Nonetheless, while the conservatives suffered losses, the sources of their power were hardly
touched, with the result that they were able, with the help of
the Dulles brothers, to organize a counter-revolution. Nor was
it possible, because of the slowness of the reforms, to create
beneficiary groups large and powerful enough to defend the
reform movement against the counter-revolution. Thus history
does not tell us whether continuation of the Arbenz reforms
would in the long run have eliminated the second danger—the
subsequent opposition of the early beneficiaries themselves.

This drag on reform emanating from the "new conservatives" appears very clearly in the Mexican Revolution. Only
fifteen years after the administration of the revolutionary General Obregon and five years after the enactment of the agrarian
measures of President Cárdenas, the reform process broke off
half way with the rise to power of the new bourgeoisie in the
administration of Miguel Aleman. Today, despite the fact that
in the 1950's Mexico had one of the world's highest industrial
and agricultural growth rates, there is little doubt that the
country is in a blind alley because of failure to solve its land
problem. Mexico's agrarian reform was the most far reaching
in Latin America before Cuba's and one which really did incorporate the peasants into national life. Nevertheless, the majority of Mexico's peasants in the *ejidos* are without resources,
while the famed economic growth concentrated in the capital
and the seven sparsely settled northern states encourages here,
as elsewhere in Latin America, speculative monoculture for export and gains tremendous earnings for the children of the
Revolution. For example, the son of the same General Obregon

is now governor of one of the northern states and the owner of more than 7,500 acres of land irrigated at government expense. The gap between the capital and the seven northern states on the one hand and the rest of the country on the other keeps growing, while the class distribution of income becomes more and more unequal. Thus, it appears that in Mexico, no less than in those countries of Latin America which have not even started their land reforms, the standard of living of the poor is going down. And that same social mobility which is both cause and effect of the integration of the peasants into national life often turns them into conservatives whose interests are opposed to the extension of the same benefits to others.*

Other land reforms, such as those of Eastern Europe after World War I, of Bolivia, and of Egypt, confirm the dangers of the second type. In each case, reform governments proceeded more or less along the lines often proposed by progressives today. The reforms were introduced slowly within the existing structure of society, and the foundations of the power of the conservatives were left intact. I do not think it is an exaggeration to say that to date all of these attempts at land reform have failed, and it is to be expected that future attempts of the second type will likewise fail.

The experience of those countries which have had successful land reforms also attests to the faults of the second and the need for the third type of reform. The outstanding examples of relative success with land reform are to be found in the socialist countries. In China and Cuba, for example, the entire structure of society was, of course, changed at the very beginning, at the same time that the land reform was initiated. This change was effected, significantly, by mobilizing the peasants themselves, and the ability of the conservatives to oppose the reforms was cut off at the root by the elimination of the sources of their power. It is true that Japan and Taiwan have had a measure of success with land reforms without at the same time radically altering the structure of their societies. But these are the kinds of exceptions which prove the rule. In

*For a fuller discussion of the Mexican case, see Andrew Gunder Frank, "Mexico: the Janus Faces of 20th Century Bourgeois Revolution," *MR,* November, 1962.

both cases, the reforms were put through relatively quickly and under the authority of an occupying military power. In these circumstances, the strength of the conservative opposition was effectively neutralized.

It might seem that as far as Latin America is concerned, the change in social structure and the elimination of conservative power which are the distinguishing features of the third type of reform would result automatically from the liquidation of the *latifundismo,* often described as a feudal or semi-feudal institution. This seems to be the way matters are seen by the architects of the Alliance for Progress. But reality is different. Although it is true that there still exist landowning sectors in Latin America which might be called feudal or semi-feudal, and that there are landowners who still hold provincial political power, it is not the case that these groups are the politically decisive ones at the national level in any Latin American country. There, political and economic power is in the hands of others—of the domestic bourgeoisies of commerce, banking, and industry, and of the great foreign corporations.

These are the important conservers of the status quo; and they and the feudal-type landowners still mutually serve each other's interests in many Latin American countries. The capitalists who have ultimate power permit the "feudalists" to survive, thus sacrificing some rural markets. But in return the feudalists, by monopolizing the land and controlling the provinces, supply the capitalists with a cheap labor force, a conservative legislature and executive, and general political "stability" and quiet in the backyard. But, as the example of Mexico so clearly shows, elimination of the feudalists does not essentially change anything because it leaves intact the power of the capitalist bourgeoisie to oppose more far-reaching agricultural reforms. This power indeed is actually enhanced if, as is usually proposed, compensation for their lands permits the feudalists to convert themselves into capitalists.

The view that Latin America is, in the words of the famous Mexican progressive novelist Carlos Fuentes, "a feudal castle with a capitalist facade" beclouds reality. The measures which the Alliance for Progress wishes to introduce, and which it hopes will substitute capitalism for feudalism, already have a century and a half of failure behind them in Latin America. It would be more accurate to say that Latin America is a capitalist castle with a feudal facade. Breaking the facade would not accomplish much, not even a land reform.

To summarize: land reform of the first type, for the benefit largely of the landowners themselves, is no reform at all. Land reform of the second type, undertaken largely by the bourgeoisie in its own interest, also holds little promise. Only land reform accompanied by a socialist transformation of society really works and is worthy of the name. Effective land reform cannot be made by conservatives or even against conservatives. It can be made only *without* conservatives.

# A GREAT AMERICAN

## BY PAUL M. SWEEZY

Most North Americans—to use the Latin American expression for the people of the United States—have probably never heard of Lázaro Cárdenas. And most of those who have heard of him probably think of him as a has-been who as an old man has become either a tool or a dupe of the Communists.

They could not be more wrong. The former President of Mexico (1934-1940) is a power not only in Mexico but throughout Latin America. Far from being a dupe or tool of anyone, he is a man of massive strength and independence. He is not even an old man. Relatively young when he was elected President one year after Franklin D. Roosevelt took office in the United States, Cárdenas in his mid-sixties is as vigorous and active as many a man ten years or more his junior.

Cárdenas's position in the Mexican political scene is unique and likely to remain so. Political power in Mexico is monopolized by the Party of Revolutionary Institutions (PRI) which completely dominates the government, the trade unions, and the national peasants' organization. As head of the big TVA-like project which centers on the Balsas River and reaches into eight states, Cárdenas holds one of the most important positions in the Mexican government. At the same time, as the inspirer and spiritual leader of the newly formed National Liberation Movement, he is the central figure in the only opposition which is potentially capable of transforming and revivifying Mexican political life. He is able to play this dual role only because of his commanding prestige in the country at large, and especially among the peasants. One of the great actors in the historical drama of the Mexican Revolution, Lázaro Cárdenas may yet hold in his hands the keys to his country's future.

As an interested observer of Mexican affairs for more than a quarter of a century, I have long been an admirer of General Cárdenas and hoped some day to have the honor of meeting him in person. When I was invited last summer to deliver three lectures at the School of Economics of the National University, it seemed that the opportunity might be at hand, but the General spends much of his time outside the capital and it proved impossible to find a date when he was both available and free. Invited again by the School of Economics to come to Mexico, this time to serve as a member of the examining board of a candidate for the degree of Licenciado (roughly comparable to our Ph.D.), I traveled to Mexico City late in April. General Cárdenas was in the capital and readily agreed to my request for an interview, which took place on April 25th in the office of his house in Lomas de Chapultepec on the outskirts of Mexico City. I was accompanied by Alonso Aguilar of the faculty of the School of Economics who studied in New York at Columbia during the 1940's and is now a member of the six-man directing committee of the Movement of National Liberation. Señor Aguilar acted as interpreter.

I of course knew of General Cárdenas's role in Mexican history and was aware of his pre-eminence in the eyes of his countrymen. I soon discovered, however, that I was very far from appreciating his full stature. It is a fair generalization, I suppose, that most people stop developing at a relatively early age. And men or women who reach a peak of achievement while they are still young and vigorous are quite likely in later life to look back on their lives with nostalgia, finding anticlimax in everything that has occurred since their days of glory. For these and related reasons, one expects a man in General Cárdenas's position to be more oriented to the past than to the present or the future; one expects his reminiscenses to be more interesting than his prognoses. Coming to the interview with preconceptions of this kind, I was unprepared to discover the real Lázaro Cárdenas of 1962. And as I sat, fascinated, listening to him discuss the great issues of the day, especially as they affect his country and mine, I came gradually to the realization that I was in the presence of one of the really great figures of American history—a man who one day will surely be ranked with Bolívar and Washington, with Juarez and Lincoln, with Fidel Castro and Franklin D. Roosevelt in the pantheon of the Americas.

Lomas de Chapultepec is a relatively new residential area where much building is in evidence; the houses, at least from the outside, are not unlike what one might see in an upper-class section of San Francisco or Los Angeles. General Cárdenas's house is one of these, outwardly much like its neighbors. There were a number of people outside and in the courtyard, evidently a part of the General's official establishment, but the atmosphere was quiet and unhurried. The office into which we were shown on arrival is well appointed and in excellent taste. General Cárdenas entered through a door that opens on a garden. At no time during the nearly two hours we were with him was one conscious that he is a busy man with many and varied responsibilities. No telephone rang, no secretary entered.

General Cárdenas, of heavy set and medium height, looks for all the world as though he had just stepped out of one of Rivera's murals depicting the panorama of Mexico's turbulent history. He speaks in a low voice without rhetorical mannerisms. His expression is mostly quiet and attentive, even immobile; but when he talks, an elusive smile lights up his olive-green eyes. Though he doesn't look at all like him, I was somehow reminded of Einstein. The modesty and deep humanity of the man are, as it were, a part of his appearance, and I suppose that this is what makes him look like Einstein after all.

I had indicated in advance that I would especially like to get his views on the Alliance for Progress, and he quickly expressed his agreement. But first he wanted to talk about Cuba, partly perhaps because, having read Leo Huberman's and my book Cuba: Anatomy of a Revolution, he knew of my great interest in the subject, but even more, I suspect, because he wanted to express to whatever audience he might reach through this interview his complete and unreserved solidarity with the Cuban Revolution and its leaders. There was no trace of holding back, of diplomatic circumlocution. The Cuban Revolution was right and good because it was undertaking essential social transformations, because it enjoyed the wholehearted support of the popular masses, and because its leaders were honest and dedicated men. I asked him whether Fidel's December declaration of adherence to Marxism-Leninism had given him any feelings of doubt or foreboding. Not at all, he said. Fidel had come to this position through experience, and in saying so openly before the world he was strengthening, not weakening, the Cuban Revolution.

I did not wish to question General Cárdenas about his personal political views, but I received the strong impression that experience had led him to essentially the same position as Fidel's. It is surely food for thought—especially, one would hope, in Washington—that the two greatest statesmen of contemporary Latin America, men who were brought up entirely within the confines of the Western democratic tradition and fought to the utmost to realize its ideals in practice—that such men have been led by their own full and often bitter experience to adopt the world outlook of revolutionary Marxism. Could there be more eloquent testimony, I thought as I listened to him speak, to the truth and universality of Marxism in the 20th century?

I asked General Cárdenas if he thought any Latin American government would dare to support openly a new U.S. attempt to overthrow Castro by armed force. He replied that there were undoubtedly several that would like to but that if they did they would not only face the overwhelming opposition of their own people but would probably find themselves threatened from neighboring countries as well. Many people from all over Latin America, he said, would sacrifice their lives in defense of Cuba even if military defeat were absolutely certain. Statements like this reflect the fact that in relation to the great issues of our time, the boundaries between Latin American countries mean very little. All Latin Americans, revolutionary and counter-revolutionary alike, feel that what happens in Cuba concerns them almost as much as it does the Cubans. As the title of a book just published in Mexico puts it, *Cuba no es una isla.*

Next we turned to the Alliance for Progress. General Cárdenas began by saying that it was quite possible that President Kennedy and others in the U.S. government are sincere in what they say about the Alliance for Progress. That is not the point. The words sound very good; the trouble is that they do not agree with the facts. There has been no progress, and nothing is being done or planned that can bring any progress. These are the facts: they are known to everyone in Latin

America. The conservatives who support the Alliance for Progress do so because it means loans from the United States. They know, and everyone else knows, that the loans come with strings attached, that their purpose is to reinforce the existing social structure, not to create the conditions necessary for progress.

I asked him whether this contradiction between words and facts, so obvious to everyone, doesn't generate enormous cynicism; whether the blatant lack of correspondence between what is said and what is done doesn't lead to distrust of words in general. He agreed that this is indeed the case: The peoples of Latin America, he said, observe that the views and attitudes of the United States agree fully with those of their own conservatives, and they know from long experience that the latter are the enemies of progress. How can they help concluding that the U.S. is also the enemy of progress? Was he not saying, I asked, that the name should be changed to the "Alliance against Progress"? He nodded assent.

There is in operation, he went on, a vicious circle. The governments of Latin America for the most part do not have the confidence of their own peoples and are not even trusted by the U.S. It follows that loans to them must be accompanied by close supervision. And this in turn offends the dignity and honor of the people who become all the more alienated from and hostile to their governments.

At this point I asked General Cárdenas if he thought it was possible for the United States to change its policies in such a way as to bring real assistance to the countries of Latin America. I mentioned the extent to which U.S. manpower is unemployed and productive capacity idle, estimating that if a real effort were made production could easily be doubled in a short time. I said that the situation seemed to many of us in the United States a disgrace at a time when so many of the people of the world are so poor and hungry. Did he think that there was any possibility that a relationship with Latin America (and other underdeveloped areas) could be worked out that would permit at least some of this unused productive power to serve the needs of the underprivileged?

It is easy to answer such a question with glib generalities

about the need for a change of heart in Washington. Present
disastrous trends can be attributed to faulty knowledge or
neglect, and the leadership of the U.S. can be exhorted to mend
its ways. We hear such diagnoses and prescription from our own
liberals every day of the week. But an answer of this kind apparently never even occurred to General Cárdenas. Rhetorical
eloquence and paper schemes for reforming the world are simply
not in his line. He is interested in knowing the truth and facing
up to it. Instead of spinning fantasies about what the U.S. might
conceivably do, he began by emphasizing what it actually is
doing. It is playing a negative role, not assisting development
but putting a brake on development. And the reason is not the
bad will or evil intent of U.S. policy-makers but the structure of
U.S. society. Those who govern an imperialist country, he was
saying in effect, will act like imperialists, and it is vain to expect
them to do otherwise.

This does not mean that General Cárdenas is at all inclined
to a fatalistic acceptance of the present pattern of relations
between the United States and Latin America. Like almost
everyone else in Latin America, he expressed bitterness at the
low and in many cases declining prices which Latin America
receives for its exports.* He deplored the lack of understanding
between people north and south of the border. Many people
in the U.S., he said, seem to think that all Mexicans are lazy.
They ought to know better. Don't many thousands of Mexicans
go to the States every year to work on farms and doesn't everyone know that they work very hard indeed? If North Americans
understood Latin America better, they would certainly bring
pressure on their government to adopt more sensible policies.
But he had no high expectations along this line. About the most

---

* On April 24th, the day before our interview, the *New York Times* car-
ried a story on the annual meeting of the Inter-American Development
Bank in Buenos Aires, which said in part: "Finance Minister Jorge Mejia
Palacio of Colombia said his country had lost two to three times as much
foreign income from falling coffee prices as it had received in Alliance for
Progress credits. He said the main thing the Alliance could accomplish
would be a long-term world coffee pact. 'Until this comes about,' Senor
Mejia asserted, 'the help that is given us, however generous it may be,
will not be blood to vitalize our economies, as was planned, but simply
tranquilizers to avoid a total collapse.' " Needless to say, the Foreign Minister of Colombia is hardly a flaming radical.

one could hope for would be that politically the U.S. would leave Latin America alone, and economically the two areas would trade more or less normally. Assistance without strings attached would be fine, but it was unlikely.

I asked General Cárdenas whether he thought that, if the United States would leave Latin America alone, revolution by peaceful, democratic means might be possible in some countries. His answer was prompt and emphatic: "No doubt about it." Keeping the present oligarchies in power cannot and will not maintain order; quite to the contrary, it will promote disorder and bloodshed. It would be vastly better if the United States would leave Latin America alone to follow its own course: without U.S. support, the position of the oligarchies would be hopeless and they would be forced to give way before popular pressures. Instead, the U.S. follows exactly the opposite course— organizing police repression, sending in money to spread corruption, building up bogeys to scare and divide people, employing the CIA to undermine and overthrow democratic movements and governments. And all of this, General Cárdenas remarked sadly, is not even in the interests of the United States: in the long run, the United States has far more to gain from decent governments and peaceful social reform in Latin America than from bloody revolutions and civil wars.

I raised the question whether ruling classes in decline could ever be expected to understand their real interests, and this led into a discussion of the general outlook for the world as a whole. Here, as elsewhere, I found that General Cárdenas had very clear and firmly held views. He expects that the Soviet Union and China (he always spoke of them together) will outstrip the United States in economic development in the years ahead, and that the underdeveloped countries will follow in their footsteps, simply because there is no other way to solve their problems. Already, the military strength of the socialist countries is so great that the United States could not possibly launch and win a war against them. For this reason, he does not believe that there will be a war. He thinks that some agreement between the United States and the Soviet Union (and China) is likely, and he hopes that a similar agreement between the United States and Latin America will eventually be possible. If only the United

States—and here I got the impression that he was thinking of the people rather than the government—would see its own interests! Because he hopes for this agreement so fervently, and because he puts more trust in peoples than in rulers, he feels that it is most important that there should be more and ever more understanding of Latin America in the United States.

I asked whether he didn't think it possible that the ruling class in the United States would refuse to accept eclipse, that sooner or later it would blow up the world rather than allow it to develop along the lines he had sketched. He didn't pretend to know. "You know your own magnates better than I do," he said. But I gathered that he didn't really believe in such a possibility. He understands the character of the age we live in with an astonishing clarity and sureness; he knows its seemingly insuperable problems, its incalculable dangers. But his commitment to humanity and his love of life are much too deep to allow him to believe in ultimate, absolute catastrophe. "In spite of all," he said, "we must be optimistic about the future."

With these words the interview came to an end. Whenever I feel discouraged by defeats or overwhelmed by the onrush of events, as surely we all must from time to time, I am going to remember them. And I am going to remember the quiet and gentle, but above all strong, man who uttered them. He is one of the great Americans of our time; his example can and should be an inspiration for all Americans whether they happen to live north or south of the Rio Grande.

# MEXICO: THE JANUS FACES OF 20th-CENTURY BOURGEOIS REVOLUTION

## BY ANDREW GUNDER FRANK

Mexico's revolutionary break with her 19th-century legacy of feudalism and imperialism, carried out at the cost of a million lives, began in 1910. Many of the political, economic, and social fruits of the Mexican Revolution were slow in ripening, and many will be gathered only in the future. From the U.S. point of view, Mexico seemed to be setting the worst kind of example to the rest of Latin America. Accordingly, the U.S. first interfered economically and diplomatically, then sent troops to capture Vera Cruz, and even as late as 1937 labeled the Mexican government "Bolshevik." At the same time, Latin America, still beset by the alliance between feudalism and imperialism, came to view the Mexican Revolution as a guiding star and shining example. By now, much has changed. Today, the U.S. is full of praise for Mexico's example of "economic progress with political stability"; and President Kennedy, indeed, is asking the Mexican government to become the pilot country in the Alliance for Progress. Latin America, in the meantime, has turned eyes toward Cuba and asks if the example of Mexico's 50-year revolution is one to follow after all. Let us, therefore, turn to the lessons that Mexico's experience holds for Latin America and the world.

The Mexican Revolution resulted in a tremendous release of popular energy, which, after the fighting ended, went into the construction of a new society. The destruction of feudalism radically changed the social relations of man to man. The peasant's accession to human dignity, when compared with the conditions of servitude which still persist in, say, Guatemala and Peru, is perhaps the Revolution's most important accomplishment. That same energy was also released through improved health (the mortality rate has fallen by two thirds since 1910)

---

Dr. Frank is a member of the social science faculty of Wayne State University in Detroit. He has recently spent long periods traveling and studying in Latin America.

and transformed into large increases of work, education (illiteracy rate reduced by one half), and skills, which in turn, particularly since 1940, have been transformed into Mexico's remarkable economic growth. Only a post- or non-feudal society could permit and produce such land reform (millions of small landholdings created), roads (sevenfold increase since 1940 so that now nearly half of all goods travel by truck and almost all passengers by bus), irrigation (an elevenfold increase since 1940 so that a third of all cropland is now irrigated), urbanization (to nearly 50 percent), industrialization (3.6-fold increase from 1940 to 1959), agricultural output (3.4-fold between 1940 and 1959); and, despite one of the world's highest rates of population growth, GNP per capita doubled from $150 to $300 a year. According to Rostow, Mexico has passed the threshold into self-sustained economic growth. Indeed, the annual rates of growth during the postwar years of both industrial and agricultural output rank Mexico among the first half-dozen countries in the world.*

And yet Mexico's revolution has had another face as well. Her crude death rate of 12.5 remains higher than that of Bolivia or Peru, her infant mortality rate of 81 in a 1000 higher than that of Argentina. Her ratio of doctors to people (1 to 2,200) is lower than Chile's and less than half of Argentina's. The 43 percent illiteracy that remained in 1950 hardly compares with 19 percent in Chile and 13 percent in Argentina. The ratio of working population engaged in manufacturing remains at 12 percent; and Mexico's per capita income of still less than $300 ranks her behind Chile, Argentina, Uruguay, and Cuba, to say nothing of oil-rich Venezuela. After the large-scale redistribution of lands, over a million heads of rural families remained without land of their own; and, with population growth, the number may have risen to nearer 2 million (out of a total of maybe 4 million) since 1950. The average Mexican diet has a caloric deficit of -24.4 according to the UN's Food and Agriculture Organization; and the 3 million indigenous Indians out of today's population of over 30 million remain economically as badly or maybe worse off than the *poorest* of

---

* A note on sources will be found at the end of the article.

their forefathers of the time before the Conquest, four and a half centuries ago. However large the social change, the economic benefits of the Mexican Revolution have not reached, or have been withheld from, large parts of the population; about 50 percent receive today only 15 percent of the national income; and it has been estimated (although also challenged) that only 1 percent of the population disposes of 66 percent of the *money* income. Further, the inequality of income distribution is increasing, not decreasing.

The wealth and elegance of downtown Mexico City dazzle the visitor, and the heavy industry of Monterrey impresses as another Pittsburgh; but equally do the miles of Mexico City's shanty slums depress, as does the poverty of rural Tlaxcala and Chiapas dumbfound. The question inevitably presents itself: have Mexico's 50 years of revolution really been a success or have they been a failure?

Compared to the experience of her closest neighbors, especially in Central America, Andean South America, and the Caribbean, Mexico's 20th century has appeared as an obvious success, the more so as these countries are only in the present decade getting ready to break the bonds that shackle them. But has the Mexican Revolution also been a failure they should seek to avoid? Economic progress in Western Europe has been greater and its benefits more widely distributed within the society. Some of the countries, small and by nature ill-endowed ones among them, have eliminated poverty entirely. True, Western Europe has in general devoted longer to the task than has Mexico, but the recent adverse change in Mexico's distribution of income raises serious doubts about her prospects of following Europe in the foreseeable future. The comparison with socialism springs to mind as well. The Soviet Union, with its revolution coming after that of Mexico, has broken all previous records by its rate of economic growth, the more so if we allow for the 10-year period of World War II and reconstruction. It may be stretching comparisons too far to apply Russia's industrial experiences to Mexico, but the USSR has eliminated illiteracy and gone on to challenge and in many ways surpass the United States in higher and technical education, providing the same opportunities to her indigenous and non-Russian-speaking peasant and nomadic peoples. And despite all agricultural difficulties, the USSR displays a similar record in the fields of nutrition, health, and medicine. More recently, China's rate of industrial growth during the past decade, and her agricultural output growth rate in the 1950's was still higher than that of Mexico. And now Cuba has eliminated her 30 percent illiteracy in a single year and nearly doubled her school enrollment in only two years since her revolution. These comparisons are no less inevitable.

Behind the two Janus faces of the Mexican Revolution there is a single head in a single and by now intricately balanced and developing organism. To learn Mexico's lesson for Latin America and the world, we must try to fathom the development, current operation, and future prospects of Mexico's revolutionary organism.

The history of Mexico seems to fall conveniently into the following periods: (1) the four centuries from the Conquest until 1910; (2) the nearly 15 years of violent revolution, counter-revolution, and reconstruction, symbolized by Madera, Huerta, and Carranza; (3) the 15 years of reform, carried through by Presidents Calles and Cárdenas; (4) the 15 years after 1940 of the beginning of industrialization and the growth of bourgeois power, symbolized by President Alemán; and (5) the current consolidation of the "Mexican System" under bourgeois leadership and the Presidency of Lopez Mateos.

At the time of the Conquest, the Spaniards found a 150-year-old Aztec empire in Central Mexico, surviving Mayan culture in the South and Yucatan, and scattered semi-nomadic tribal Indians in the North, including today's Southwestern United States. The populous Center was soon colonized by Spaniards, the existing social system largely destroyed, the Indians' labor and land exploited, and their numbers reduced by half. The more arid, less populated, and tribal North, on the other hand, was settled only gradually and sparsely, as the extension of livestock ranching and mining in that area required. This difference between the North and the populous Center and South, as will emerge later, still dominates Mexico's social and economic experience in the last 20 years of our time.

In 1810, under the leadership of the priest Hidalgo,

Mexico's peasants rebelled. Unmatched by peasant activity elsewhere in Spanish America, where peasants remained at best passive and often in support of the Spanish Crown, and unsupported by the Latin American-born Creole Spaniards, the rebellion came to nothing. Not until the landowning and particularly commercial Creoles took up the fight themselves did independence come to Mexico and the other Spanish colonies in America. Again in the 1850's, now under the leadership of the Indian Benito Juárez, the Mexicans attempted reform in their feudal structure. But after the French intervention and under the 30-year reign of Porfirio Díaz, peonage returned in full force and concentration of landownership became worse than ever. At the same time, foreign capital, increasingly American, entered the country on most favored terms until it reached over $400 million, concentrated in land, mines, and the transportation system required to ship produce abroad.

The Mexican Revolution was the product of alliance between the bourgeoisie, represented by Madera, and the peasants, led by Emiliano Zapata and Pancho Villa. They faced a common enemy, the feudal order and its supporting pillars of Church, army, and foreign capital. But their goals inevitably differed—freedom from domestic and foreign bonds and loosening of the economic structure for the bourgeoisie; land for the peasants. Although Zapata continued to press the interests of the peasants until his murder in 1919, the real leadership of the Revolution was never out of the hands of the bourgeoisie, except insofar as it was challenged by Huerta reaction and American intervention. (Even in the 1958 presidential election, only 23 percent of the population voted.) The elimination of feudal social relations was of course in the interest of the emerging bourgeoisie as well as of the peasants. Education became secularized, Church and state more widely separated. But accession to power by the peasantry was never really in the cards.

None of the early presidents were radicals in any sense of the word, nor could they have been and retained their positions. In the middle 1920's, during the administration of President Calles, there began the program of public works, and to a lesser extent irrigation, on the foundation of which much of Mexico's subsequent economic development rests. Then too were written the laws, pursuant to Article 27 of the relatively advanced Constitution of 1917, which were to guide the land reform until the 1940's. That article provided for expropriation of private lands in the public interest and for distribution of the land to neighboring villages, ranches, and communities whose supply of land is insufficient for their needs, "always respecting small property." Two important legal interpretations of this provision stand out: lands to be distributed to particular communities were to be taken from private properties exceeding certain sizes within a seven-kilometer radius of the communities; and a proportion of private land was to be expropriated corresponding to the increment in the land's value due to any irrigation or other improvements that may be undertaken by the state, thus preventing large landholders from becoming the favored beneficiaries of investments incurred at public expense.

Abroad, the Cárdenas administration (1934-1940) may be best known for its expropriation of Mexico's privately owned petroleum, a step which was also provided for by the same Article 27 of the Constitution of 1917. But still more important domestically, the administration of President Cárdenas expropriated and redistributed more land than all other administrations, before and since, put together. Pursuant to the Constitution and the laws of the Calles administration, these lands were taken from the territories surrounding particular villages and were ceded to them communally as *ejidos*, to be worked in some cases collectively but in most cases individually. An *ejido* bank was established to provide the new owners with agricultural credit. Irrigation and other capital investment in agriculture was not, however, expanded at the same time. In fact, in retrospect it is clear that, although he undoubtedly had his heart in the right place, Cárdenas, as head of a bourgeois government, did not provide Mexican peasant agriculture with nearly enough resources to get it over the hump into self-sustained development.

From a careful study of the Bajio region of Central Mexico a decade after Cárdenas, the following findings, which are not unrepresentative for Mexico as a whole, emerge about the relative resource endowments of *ejido* and small private agriculture. (I shall turn to the discussion of large-scale agriculture when I come to the postwar period.) Relative to private farmers, *ejidatarios* have less land (3.8 as against 16.5 hectares per man); more third-quality and less first-quality land; less education (about one tenth of their school-age children in primary school as against one half for the private farmers); more reliance on family and female labor; female labor employed relatively more in cultivation and less in administration; less reliance on outside and permanently hired labor; more unemployment (85 percent of the total); less investment in irrigation (private farmers have 35 percent more irrigated surface and use 65 percent more water); less capital (40 percent of the amount that private owners have, although there are three times as many *ejidatarios*); more dependence on almost exclusively public credit and outside capital supplies, while private farmers have access to a much larger supply of private credit.

With such handicaps, it is perhaps no wonder that many *ejidatarios* have been unable to provide themselves with a decent living. Indeed, in several respects the situation is even worse than that described, and it appears that the political and economic structure that emerged from the Revolution was not really designed to, and does not, permit the large mass of peasants to share in its economic fruits. We should remember that more than a million, now approaching two million, rural family heads remain entirely landless.

Public agricultural credit accounts for no more than a third of all agricultural credit, and about half of that is supplied not by the Ejido Bank but by the Agricultural Bank which lends to large private landholders. Oscar Lewis quotes the research director of the Ejido Bank: "We lend to about one third of all *ejidatarios,* those that have the richest and best lands. We prefer risks that have fertile soil and preferably irrigation. We do not have enough money for loans to subsistence farmers most of whom have the poorest lands." But private credit reaches the *ejidatario* still less; and much of it, like the 2.5 billion pesos annually lent to cotton growers by the American concern of Anderson and Clayton (compared to the 1.5 billion pesos lent by the Ejido Bank to all *ejidatarios* combined), is earmarked for special purposes.

For lack of working capital, many *ejidatarios* have found it necessary to lease their newly won land to private holders in command of capital and then to turn around and work for these capitalist farmers as hired laborers on their *own* land. Other *ejidatarios* and landless peasants, as is well known, find it necessary each year to migrate to the United States by the hundreds of thousands to work as migratory agricultural laborers there; or they emigrate to the growing city slums in search of work.

How then, we may well ask, has Mexico been able to show the increases of agricultural and industrial output that were cited previously, if it now appears that the economic condition of the bulk of her population has scarcely improved? Much of the answer emerges from the data collected by Paul L. Yates for his important study of regional economic development in Mexico. After the expiration of Cárdenas's term in the Presidency, and particularly with the accession of Miguel Alemán between 1946 and 1952, the bulk of investment went into the North and the Federal District. As we have already noted, the seven Northern states have traditionally had less of the total population, a lower population density, and a smaller percentage of the labor force engaged in agriculture than the heart of Mexico. While per capita investment remained well under 1,000 pesos for the period 1946-1955 in the 10 least favored states, it rose to well above 5,000 in the 7 Northern states and the Federal District. The difference in funds devoted to irrigation between the North and the rest of the country is even more striking, with 60 percent of all irrigation investment between 1947 and 1958 going to the three states Baja California del Norte, Sonora, and Tamaulipas alone. As a result, much of the increase in Mexico's sown area was concentrated in the relatively less populated North as well. The same area also absorbed the bulk of the increase of agricultural credit and virtually all mechanized farm equipment (an increase in the number of tractors from 4,620 in 1940 to 55,000 in 1955) that was not devoted to the production of sugar, another non-subsistence crop, in the South. Not one tractor was used on any of the million small holdings in 1950. Not surprisingly, agricultural output (though not income) rose in the North to state averages of 12,000, 20,000, and even 34,000 pesos per agricultural worker in 1960; while it remained at levels of 2,000 and 3,000 pesos in the older states.*

This growth in agricultural output, however, was concentrated in industrial crops, principally cotton, the production of which rose 309 percent between 1939 and 1954, while that of food crops rose only 113 percent. Moreover, the bulk of these crops—cotton, vegetables, sugar (Center and Yucatan), coffee (Chiapas), and livestock—were destined for export to the North American market. The earnings from this agricultural export were used variously: some were ploughed back into the same export agriculture; some were invested in industry; some were consumed (we will turn later to the resulting distribution of income); and some, unfortunately for Mexico as for other countries exporting primary goods, were left in the importing country because of the decline, particularly after the Korean War, of raw material prices relative to those of industrial goods.

The exigencies of World War II had given impetus to domestic expansion of industry in Mexico as elsewhere in the underdeveloped world. Further industrialization was promoted by Alemán and his successors. Investment in industry and commerce has also been guided into the same eight favored states, with particular concentrations, of course, in the Federal District and Nuevo Leon, the sites of Mexico City and Monterrey. The older, more populated states were left largely unaffected and far behind. A significant portion of the investment funds, and particularly of the necessary foreign exchange, undoubtedly was contributed by the earnings from agricultural exports as well as from the rapid increase of tourism in Mexico and migrant bracero labor to the United States. But simultaneously, American direct investment which had fallen to the depression and post-petroleum-nationalization low of $267 million in 1939 began again a rapid increase and now surpasses the $1 billion mark, or about one tenth of U.S. investment in Latin America. This American investment has displayed a relative shift away from "social overhead" capital and into manufacturing and trade, so that in 1953, of the 31 companies with a gross annual income exceeding 100 million pesos, 19 were U.S. owned or

---

* One U.S. dollar equals 12.5 pesos.

controlled, 5 were in the hands of the Mexican government, and only 7 were private domestic firms. Moreover, since the ownership certificates of Mexican enterprises are bearer and not name bonds and shares, and since after issuance these certificates typically tend to gravitate into the hands where capital is already concentrated, it is not always easy to determine where ownership, and particularly control lies. Thus, U.S. control of Mexican industry today may well be close to 50 percent. Against this background, it is not surprising to hear the Mexican Chamber of Manufacturing Industries say that "the economic power of these large foreign enterprises constitutes a serious threat to the integrity of the nation and to the liberty of the country to plan its own economic development."

In Mexican agriculture as well, American capital plays a significant role. Although Americans no longer own large tracts of land, as they still do in Central America, the American cotton monopoly, Anderson and Clayton, as already noted, distributes about $200 million of credit for the production of cotton from sowing to shipping. Therewith it effectively determines the buyer and the price for the cotton and prevents Mexico from disposing of a large part of her cotton crop where and when she might wish. And worse, as we shall see below, this arrangement contributes to the maintenance of monoculture and a plantation economy using hired labor in large parts of the North. With good reason, "Mexicans are beginning to wonder whether they are returning to the days of Porfirio Díaz."

The relative effects of events since World War II on the Mexican South and North have already emerged from the foregoing discussion. They are perhaps best summarized by indexes of social welfare presented in the table on page 380.

But much of the detail of the emerging allocation of resources and distribution of income remains hidden behind the regional averages to which the table is necessarily limited. To expose more, it is necessary to inquire into the organization of political and economic power and how it has developed since the days of Cárdenas. When Alemán launched his campaign of large-scale irrigation and industrialization, he also introduced some legal changes. Recall the two provisions of Article 27 of the Constitution that have already been cited in discussing the ad-

ministrations of Presidents Calles and Cárdenas. These provisions, referring to the distribution of land as *ejidos* contiguous
to the communities that were to receive them and allowing expropriation only with due respect to small property, were to
receive, under the guidance of Alemán, a significance quite
contrary to what they had had before—and quite other, one
might suspect, from what the framers of the Constitution had
intended.

With respect to the first provision, it must be remembered
that the Northern states are sparsely populated and contain vast
areas in which there were no settled communities. When lands
in such areas were opened to cultivation through irrigation,

### INDEXES OF SOCIAL WELFARE
(National Average=100)

|  | Mortality Reciprocal[a] | Running Water | Literacy | General Welfare |
|---|---|---|---|---|
| *Eight Most Favored States* | | | | |
| Baja Calif. No. | 160 | 127 | 145 | 204 |
| Dist. Fed. | 124 | 215 | 145 | 188 |
| Sonora | 106 | 97 | 128 | 157 |
| Nuevo Leon | 136 | 115 | 139 | 144 |
| Baja Calif. Sur | 123 | 92 | 138 | 148 |
| Tamaulipas | 134 | 123 | 132 | 136 |
| Coahuila | 108 | 132 | 130 | 136 |
| Chihuahua | 103 | 104 | 128 | 147 |
| *Ten Least Favored States* | | | | |
| Chiapas | 91 | 80 | 61 | 52 |
| Oaxaca | 75 | 65 | 64 | 43 |
| Tabasco | 95 | 45 | 102 | 70 |
| Tlaxcala | 83 | 66 | 97 | 60 |
| Guerrero | 115 | 75 | 55 | 58 |
| Hidalgo | 74 | 84 | 71 | 65 |
| Querétaro | 83 | 81 | 62 | 70 |
| Guanajuato | 82 | 76 | 77 | 65 |
| Zacatecas | 107 | 70 | 105 | 56 |
| Michoacan | 115 | 70 | 105 | 54 |

a. This index is so constructed that a *lower* mortality rate yields a *higher*
index figure.

*Source*: Paul L. Yates, El Desarrollo Regional de Mexico, *passim.*

*Note*: The eight favored states are all at the northern boundary of Mexico,
except for the Federal District which is the site of the capital. Least
favored states are in the Center and South. Altogether, there are 29 states
in addition to two territories and the Federal District. The General Welfare index is a composite constructed by Yates.

Article 27 was interpreted as excluding, or at least not requiring, their distribution as *ejidal* lands. At the same time, the Constitutional provision for due regard to "small property" now came, under a Law of Inaffectability, to be interpreted as excluding 100 hectares of irrigated, 150 hectares of ordinary, and more of grazing land from expropriation. Accordingly, existing private owners of larger tracts of relatively worthless land in the North, on learning of prospective state irrigation projects in their areas, rushed to "sell" their holdings in plots of the minimum inaffectable acreage to all available members of their families. The result was twofold: not only did they retain effective control of much of their lands—as an example, the son of a revolutionary general and President, himself now governor of a Northern state, is reputed to own 3,000 hectares of irrigated land in three estates—but they also reaped the benefit of the always large and often astronomical increase in its value due to the state-financed irrigation. Thus, they rendered inoperative the letter and intent of the earlier Calles law which was meant to channel the benefits of state-financed irrigation to the public at large. Instead, under the Alemán law, their lands had become inalienable! The legal assessments to the private owners to siphon off the increase in land values were and are more often than not essentially disregarded. In this manner, according to the 1950 Census, while *ejidal* holdings increased 21 percent, and small private holdings increased 20 percent, the larger private landholdings rose by 48 percent; and the share of landholdings larger than 5 hectares in the total of all cropland rose from 39 percent to 43 percent. The real amount of land which is effectively in large holdings is, however, undoubtedly greater and unknown because the census classification cannot adequately distinguish between actually and fictitiously separate landholdings. The matter appears to be further complicated by the holdings of livestock grazing lands, and it is placed entirely beyond inspection if we refer to *values,* and their spectacular increase, rather than to mere acreage.

The foregoing events of the postwar years have had their inevitable effect on the socio-political and economic structure of the society and on the lives of the people within it. They have meant the growth of a neo-latifundia agriculture, no longer

organized under the feudal *hacienda* system which uses serfs to
produce for home consumption, but organized instead as latter-
day plantations, run as capitalist enterprises by city-dwelling
owners, hiring agricultural wage laborers, and producing non-
subsistence and often single crops for export.

The Northern states have thus become magnets of in-
migration of *ejidal* or landless peasants who leave their villages
in the Center and South. This movement contributes somewhat
to redressing the balance of income distribution, for the agricultural workers of the North are economically somewhat better
off than their *ejidal* and landless brother in the South. The
tabular index of social welfare in terms of regions, however,
probably results in a considerable overstatement of the Northern
advantage if it is read not as a regional but as a personal difference between the farmer North and South, for the regional
figure is probably heavily weighted also by the income dif-
ferential between bourgeois and peasant. A trip through the
North readily suggests that large masses of its inhabitants are
not sharing its prosperity.

The new private landowners, large and small, and some of
the old ones as well, are or are becoming bourgeois in every sense
of the word. Even the smaller landowners among them, if they
have any capital, have a position and income which affords
them a middle-class style of life, and often urban life at that.
Their agricultural business often affords them a handsome income, which they dispose of sometimes by real investment in
Mexico, sometimes by investment abroad, sometimes by con-
structing and speculating in urban real estate, or luxury imports.
And they have power, economic and political. They and their
industrial, commercial, and sometimes professional brethren
essentially own and run the state. Beginning particularly during
the administration of Alemán, they have, as we have seen in
part, been able to use that state to pull themselves up by their
bootstraps. But it has not, so far, been their interest to pull the
peasantry up behind them. Is it any wonder that, according to
Mrs. Navarete's recent study of income distribution, the share
of the total national income going to the richest 20 percent of
families rose from 59.8 percent in 1950 to 61.4 percent in

1957, while that of the poorest 50 percent dropped from 18.1 percent to 15.6 percent?

It remains to ask how the "Mexican System" works today under the administration of President Lopez Mateos and what are its prospects for the future. Mexico is a social and economic pyramid, with a political pyramid inside. At the bottom are the indigenous Indians, remaining where they always were. In the next layer are the landless rural people and the unemployed or only occasionally employed urban ones. The latter, particularly, are a veritable *lumpenproletariat*, dispossesed by the rural and unabsorbed by the urban economy, living on the margin of society, isolated and alienated from it, from each other, and often from themselves. Next come the *ejidatarios* and such private small holders as are poor enough to work their land by themselves. Although economically more secure, they stand socially sometimes even below the marginal urban people, perhaps because the *chances* for social mobility are greater for the latter. Above them are the workers in the narrower sense of the word, particularly the unionized ones, who in Mexico as in many parts of Latin America, Asia, and Africa today comprise a sort of "aristocracy of the proletariat." The next layer may be termed the middle class or petty bourgeoisie. It comprises a large variety of economic walks of life—small landowner, professional, merchant, clergy, government and white collar worker, small politician—but it affords considerable lateral mobility within it, from one occupation to another. Their badge in Mexico is dark glasses as it is a briefcase in Western Europe, however dark it may be outside or however few papers there may be to carry. And that badge is a counterweight to the sometimes higher income of the workers below them. The bourgeois upper class, the principal manipulators and beneficiaries of the system, includes the large landholders, the effective directors of the financial commercial, industrial, professional, governmental, and military apparatuses, and by *noblesse oblige* some intellectuals. The viable economic base of the more aristocratic upper class was destroyed by the Revolution. But many of its members and their wealth survived. Their money was invested in finance, commerce, industry, and later again agriculture; and the ex-aristocrats became the nucleus of the new bourgeoisie. Their ranks were soon supplemented by their erstwhile enemies, the individual beneficiaries of the same Revolution, many politicians and generals among them. As their economic position became consolidated, so did their political power—exercised through the PRI, the all-powerful Institutional Revolutionary Party through which they have managed Mexico's political, and thereby indirectly economic, life for the past generation. It is the PRI which allocates the presidency and other principal political offices (to its faithful), and not the electoral mechanism; and management and control of the PRI, in turn, by no means extends down to the bottom of the social and economic pyramid.

But Mexico's pyramid is not static; it is not a caste system, as for example that of Peru substantially remains; there is mobility. There are economic, political, and social paths which afford opportunities—or, maybe better, chances—for higher rank to those who play according to the rules of the game. There is the migration from Center and South to the North, involving as it does not only geographical movement but also economic improvement coupled with some severance of communal ties and participation in a looser society. There is the very substantial rural-urban migration, especially to Mexico City which grew from 1.4 million and 7 percent of the population in 1940 to over 4 million and 13 percent today. Of course, such migration offers no guarantee of social or economic success, but it increases the statistical chances for the migrant. There is movement into white or off-white collar jobs and various kinds of speculation around the loose ends of a growing economy. And, of course, there is education and "suitable" marriage for those who can manage it. These two are perhaps the most important vehicles for the social and economic migrant himself, and virtually guarantee mobility to his children.

Social mobility, however, is individual-by-individual. Individuals, some of them, are permitted, indeed encouraged, to "better themselves," but within the system and according to its rules. In fact, the "System" and the Party co-opt people into their ranks to obviate their rocking the boat. Perhaps most symbolic of this process is the recent invitation by President Lopez Mateos to the seven living ex-Presidents, and their acceptance, to join his administration in semi-official, semi-honorary positions, a step that was taken to help stabilize the political situation in Mexico "after Cuba." In more pedestrian ways, labor leaders, popularly called *charros,* are co-opted into the business system and rewarded, to keep unions from rocking the boat. Even young Marxists can hope to attain positions of responsibility in later years and may therefore turn to defend the system. Indeed, the Mexican Communist Party is sometimes called Mexico's leading school for conservatives. Most important, the social structure and its mythology have given the lower-middle class, and even people in the lower class, the feeling that it is possible to rise up, partly in and partly with, the system.

While mobility individual-by-individual is permitted, mobility by group is not. If group pressure begins to build up anywhere in the politico-economic system, the first step, as suggested above, is to co-opt or recruit away the leadership. Additionally, small concessions may be used to abate the pressure and take the wind out of the movement's sails. Thus, for instance, the price of corn (*maiz*) and movies (!) is subsidized in the City of Mexico, some will say to help the poor and others to ward off popular unrest. Similarly, after substantial popular pressure had built up, President Lopez Mateos recently created some livestock *ejidos* in the North; however, he has yet to grant a single acre of irrigated land to an *ejido.* If these measures are not successful, the government finally resorts to repression. Strikes, particularly those with political overtones, such as those of the most militant among unions, the railroad workers' three years ago, and the teachers' last year, have been severely dealt with. Particularly since the increase of liveliness in political life and the full-scale introduction of the Cold War after the Cuban Revolution, left-wing labor leaders and others have increasingly found themselves sitting in jail. To prove that no one, no matter what his status, is immune from this fate, Mexico's most famous living painter, the 65-year-old internationally known David Alfaro Siqueiros and his 73-year-old friend, the noted journalist Filomena Mata, are in jail on 8-year (!) sentences for allegedly having caused the teachers' union, of which they are not even members, to go on strike. The official charge is threatening "social dissolution," whatever that may mean. On the other hand, rightist influence, even on the part of the Church whose wings had been clipped 100 and again 50 years ago, has been steadily growing and consolidating itself.

Thus the System offers glory to some individuals, bread and circuses, often more circuses than bread, to the masses—supposedly ample rewards for repudiating militant leadership. Occasional economic, but no political concessions, are offered when necessary, and repression is resorted to if all else fails. On the whole, the System seems to work quite well: it is significant that Mexico devotes only 8 percent of her national budget to the army, compared to Colombia's 30 percent or Haiti's 45 percent; only relatively middle-class Costa Rica among the Latin American countries spends less. But it is also true that the System withholds real participation and benefits from the bulk of the Mexican people.

What are the prospects for the future? Industrialization, rapid as it has been, education, capitalization of agriculture, public works, and other "modernization" measures have not so far been sufficient really to absorb the population increase, let alone greatly to raise the economic level of the peasant base. Moreover, the present government has reduced Alemán's annual irrigation expenditures by nearly half; and the spectacular 8-10 percent rate of GNP increase of the mid-1950's has steadily declined to an alarming zero percent last year. With the existing economic organization and structure of bourgeois political and economic power, and the relative increase of private over public investment in recent years, there is enough reason to doubt that the Mexican economy will soon afford the bulk of its people a significantly better standard of life. It certainly does not promise the economic and cultural advances shown in this century, and particularly since World War II by the socialist countries. Yet, as we have seen, the System does lumber along, as those of Guatemala, Peru, yes, of Venezuela and Colombia, to say nothing of several other Latin American countries, no longer do. And it makes adjustments here and there. As the economy proceeds by co-optation, so does the political system and its political party, only more so. Nothing seems to be possible working from outside the PRI; and everything that is possible can be attained only by joining and working through the PRI. The office of the President is all-powerful no matter who fills it: it is more than a literary or journalistic quirk that Mexicans have transformed the names of their Presidents into nouns and adjectives for use in referring to their administrations, nay epochs. And an ex-President counts for no more than anyone else without political access to the current incumbent.

Thus, although Cárdenas, apparently spurred on by the Cuban Revolution, recently emerged from 20-year political retirement to join younger men in founding the MLN (National Liberation Movement) which is designed to mobilize and unify Mexico's political Left, he nevertheless accepted the invitation to ex-Presidents to join the Lopez Mateos administration along with his more conservative colleagues. It is no wonder the Left is disunited, nay fractionated; and the birth of the MLN is maybe more a sign of the need for unity on the Left than of its achievement. At the same time, the current wave of governmental repression against the Left need not mean a permanent move to the Right. As Latin America as a whole moves further to the Left in the coming years, the pressure on Mexico may become so great the Mexican Left will again have its day (helped along by U.S. repressive acts designed to prevent it)—but working within and through the PRI. Pablo Gonzales Casanova, Dean of the always progressive School of Political and Social Sciences at the National University and prominent member of the MLN suggests: "We think that General Lázaro Cárdenas has indicated the right road: support the institution and organize the people."

It is easy to concur with this judgment. But organize the people for what? Only to wrest the control of their destinies away from the bourgeoisie and the PRI? While the Mexican people "organize," other Latin Americans will inevitably make revolutions far more radical than that of Mexico. As the Cuban Revolution has already done, these revolutions abroad will just as inevitably sharpen the antagonisms between the Left and Right in Mexico itself. Any short-run, moderate gains the Mexican Left can achieve within the present system by riding on the wave of social revolution among her neighbors, can only postpone the day when the Mexican Left must radically break the power of the bourgeoisie, and begin itself to direct Mexico's destiny.

## A Note On Sources

The foregoing article is based in part on personal observation and inquiry and in part on published materials. In addition to Mexican newspapers and such U.S. press organs as the *New York Times* and *Time,* the following were the chief sources relied upon:

Casanova, Pablo Gonzales, "Mexico: El Ciclo de una Revolucion Agraria," *Cuadernos Americanos,* Jan.-Feb., 1962.

Castillo, Carlos Manuel, "La Economia Agricola e la Region del Bajio," *Problemas Agricolas e Industriales,* VIII, No. 3-4, 1956.

Lewis, Oscar, "Mexico Since Cárdenas," in Richard N. Adams and others, *Social Change in Latin America Today: Its Implications for United States Policy,* Vintage Books, New York, 1961.

Yates, Paul Lamartine, *El Desarrollo Regional de Mexico,* Banco de Mexico, 1961.

# VENEZUELA: A STUDY IN IMPERIALISM

## BY HARVEY O'CONNOR

For Venezuelans, the dread words that wrote themselves on the wall at Belshazzar's feast, "Mene, mene, tekel upharsin," have a special meaning. In the Indian language of that country, "mene" means oil.

Some 10 percent of Venezuela is sitting in on the modern Belshazzar's feast, catered by Standard Oil and Shell; the other 4,000,000 are on the outside looking in, with hunger in their bellies and disease in their bones. But some day, when the last oil is pumped out, the feast must end.

Then, in the words of Arturo Uzlar-Pietri, the stricken land will need the disaster services of International Red Cross brigades doling out soup as its people expire surrounded by mountains of empty Frigidaires, silent Philcos, and gasless Cadillacs. Prophet of doom, Uzlar-Pietri is also a leading economist, a minister in former governments, professor at the University of Caracas, popularizer of the slogan "sembrar el petroleo"— invest the income from oil royalties in rehabilitation of the nation.

Uzlar-Pietri is not alone in his jeremiads. From right to left and deep in the center, Venezuela's economists know that its present prosperity is as stable as the pool of oil it sits on. They know that the heart of the country is being eaten out, even as the skyscrapers rise higher in Caracas and the chrome-plated suburbs reach up and down the valley high in the Andes.

When oil was discovered along Lake Maracaibo, Venezuela was a sleepy, provincial, semi-feudal land of 2 million feeding itself somehow and exporting annually $20 million of coffee, cocoa, and cattle. After 25 years of oil prosperity, Venezuela's

Harvey O'Connor is the author of *Mellon's Millions, The Guggenheims, The History of the Oil Workers International Union,* and other books. He has recently returned from several months of investigating conditions in the Caribbean area.

exports (aside from oil) are still $20 million a year, mainly coffee and cocoa. There are no surplus cattle left to export, and were it not for government subsidies, not a single bean of coffee or cocoa could enter the world market.

After a quarter century of oil imperialism, Venezuela can no longer feed herself. According to Dr. Miguel Parra Leon, another eminent Venezuelan economist, the country now produces only half the corn, half the meat, one-third of the green vegetables and grains, and half the milk it consumes. There are fewer cattle on the great llanos that sweep to the Orinoco than at the time of the Revolution in 1812.

The most widely advertised commodity is "Klim," a powdered milk imported from Wisconsin. Fresh milk is flown in daily from Miami. Two hundred thousand peasants who have deserted their "conucos" and the plantations now live under the bridges in golden Caracas, or along the gullies or up on the hillsides above the city, in ironically named "ranchos." These "ranchos" are devoid of streets, sewers, water, light, schools, or any amenity. Shacks made of packing boxes, discarded tin sheet, wall board, and burlap "house" one-third of the city.

Only oil really "grows." If the fields are being deserted, and the llanos are empty of cattle, the factories are certainly artificial. Not one would survive lowering of the tariff wall, for any manufactured article can be bought more cheaply in New York, London, or Amsterdam than it can be made in Venezuela.

In general, everything in Venezuela except primitive products costs 50 to 100 percent more than in the States. If it is imported, it costs the New York price, plus transportation to La Guaira, plus heavy import duties and harbor fees, plus transportation to the capital, plus importer's mark-up, plus wholesaler's mark-up, plus retailer's mark-up. If produced domestically, then the price is the sum of the New York price on similar merchandise, plus the tariff wall, plus profits. Whatever may be the pleasures of Caracas, they are not for American tourists, who would shy away from the Andean price level; even the local bourgeoisie saves money by spending longish seasons in Miami, New York, or Paris.

Profits are enormous. So much money can be made so easily in Caracas real estate that a speculator would be a fool to piddle around with 10-20 percent profits in industry and commerce. Fifty percent seems to be the minimum acceptable. A glass bottle factory was dismantled because it made only 80 percent, and there was bigger money to be made elsewhere. (The United States bottle industry was of course interested in the dismantling.) This is no "normal" capitalist economy, but one geared to speculation and quick riches.

What has happened to Venezuela is a gold-plated disaster moving on noiseless oiled bearings toward tragedy. Its ancient, static but self-sufficient economy has been tossed in the ashcan. Now it reaps billions of bolívars each year for its oil. With these bolívars it buys all the expensive trash of the world—baubles, Uzlar-Pietri calls them. When the oil runs out, he says, the nation will be like an old tailor's chest filled with useless spangles. Lacking subsidies, industry will collapse; agriculture will long since have perished.

"The monoproductive character of the exploitation in Latin America whether in oil, bananas, or minerals," writes a Venezuelan student in New York, "chokes the free development of our national economy by making the state dependent on that income. Therefore it is impossible to diversify and the large commercial interests and the landlords become happy parasites on what is handed out to them; the peasantry and the workers are further impoverished and the semi-feudal framework remains unchanged."

No colonial country can rival Venezuela's top-heavy economy. Oil represents 94 percent of her exports. At least three-fourths of the government's $500 million-a-year income is attributed to oil.

The rise of oil has been meteoric. In 1917, only 121 thousand barrels were produced along Lake Maracaibo. In 1928 the figure was 105 million; in 1940, 183 million. By 1949 it had leaped up to 475 million.

The effect on the federal budget has also been meteoric. In 1917, the government operated on an income of $20 million, including $50,000 in oil taxes. Twenty years later, the income was $100 million, with oil furnishing $25 million. But last year government revenues were $525 million. Of this, $177 million came from oil royalties, $97 million from import duties financed almost wholly through oil exports, $76 million from income taxes, again mostly oil-produced, and $60 million from profit on dollar-bolívar exchange, almost wholly due to oil. So the economy of Venezuela is a "budget economy"; the government seems to be the source of all wealth, although in reality it merely redistributes the income it gets from oil.

If the oil revenues seem generous, that is a tribute to the world's most far-sighted and ably-led corporation—Standard Oil of New Jersey. Standard wants no Iran in Venezuela. It is a privilege and a pleasure to pay so much to the government— or so little, when it is remembered that Standard's Venezuela subsidiary, Creole, made a profit of $167 million last year. This figures out at $9,630 on the labor of each of its employes— probably the world's record, and another tribute to Standard's sagacity.

Standard produces about half of all Venezuela's oil. Shell, the British-Dutch company, accounts for a fourth, Gulf (Mene Grande) for a seventh. The rest is produced by other American companies such as Socony (another Standard firm), Sinclair, and Phillips.

The military Junta holds the reins, but need it be added that Arthur T. Proudfit, head of Creole, holds the power? The relationship is subtle and implicit. Mr. Proudfit thunders no orders, pounds no tables in Caracas. In the pillaging of a nation, both sides understand that a suave cordiality based on a fair division of the swag is what counts. For this, Creole pays over royalties and taxes, on a 50-50 basis on its profits; for this, the Junta pays $50 million a year to maintain its ministry of national defense. As no other Latin nation wants to invade Venezuela, the national defense money can be devoted entirely to police, jails, spies, and the paraphernalia of internal suppression.

In the presence of the majestic profits of the corporations and the lordly income of the Junta, it would be ungenerous to stint the workers. Venezuelan oil workers earn more than their brothers in any land except the United States. They are paid for seven days of the week, buy in company-subsidized commissaries, have company-provided hospital and medical services, live in company houses, send their children to company schools, and enjoy 25 days of paid vacation each year.

The labor and social security laws in many respects are more advanced than in the United States. Based on the ability of the oil corporations to pay, on the struggles of the unions, and on the liberal outlook of Acción Democrática, these laws set minimum wages, provide two weeks' paid vacations for all workers each year, one month's severance pay for each year worked, full pay for Sundays and holidays not worked, and 10 percent of the net profits paid as a special bonus at the end of the year. Minimum wages range from $1.20 a day for unskilled jobs in smaller cities to $9 for skilled work in Maracaibo, the oil capital. Union scales are higher.

The other side of the picture shows the countryside drained of its most vigorous youth who flow to the oil camps and the cities to try to get into the magic circle of oil. It shows housing without amenities, except in the oil camps; a diet that leaves lingering disease unchecked; social conditions which encourage gambling, prostitution, and the consumption of aguardiente. The erosion that is tearing away the country's best soil is matched by the human erosion in the Anzóategui oil camps, where 22 percent of the workers suffer major accidents each year, leading to death or permanent or partial disability, while a third suffer serious accidents.

Two-thirds of the people live in the countryside. Some work for wages on the plantations (latifundias), but most are share-cropperrs or till their own little "conucos," mere clearings torn out of the mountainsides and deserted when the soil washes down the gullies. Only 10 percent of the rural population own their own land. Four percent of the rural population own 78 percent of the cultivable soil. These are the latifundias, which produce what remains of the export crops. The "conucos" do not even furnish a subsistence, so the conuquero must hire himself out to get the ready cash needed for clothing and for his family's needs.

This is the "real" Venezuela—there before oil was struck, there now, and all that will remain when oil is gone. It was impoverished, disease-ridden, illiterate 25 years ago, and still is.

This is the Venezuela which anguishes patriots who regard the country's prosperity as an illusion. This is the one-fifth of the nation where four-fifths of the people live, for most of Venezuela is still an untapped wilderness. The great llanos that stretch from the Andes to the Orinoco support less life today than a hundred years ago; the Guayana highlands beyond the Orinoco are inhabited only by primitive forest Indians.

The land is the country's central problem, but no one dares to touch it. Acción Democrática passed an agrarian reform law in 1945 but was afraid to implement it. Some land was rented from the latifundistas and sub-rented to peasants, and that was all.

Salvador de la Plaza, Venezuela's leading Marxist economist, a bitter critic of the inept Acción Democrática, has sketched the agrarian reform the land needs. He calls for dispossession of the latifundistas, the organizing of peasant communes, the provision of adequate credits, machinery, technical services, and social amenities.

For once, the problem is not lack of economic means. The majestic income from oil could easily finance the rejuvenation of Venezuela's agriculture in less than a generation. The money is there, but not the will—at least so far as the government is concerned.

The country does not lack for planners. Nearly every economist has tried his hand at it, and the present Minister of International Development (Fomento), Manuel R. Egaña, is no exception. On paper he has sketched the spending of billions of dollars. He would "sow the petroleum" dollars in this way: $300 million for harbors and canals, $600 million for roads, $600 million for irrigation and electrification. It is a typical bourgeois economist's dream. The harbors are to be enlarged so that Venezuela can import more food, more autos, more electric refrigerators. Already the ports of La Guaira and Puerto Cabello are choked with these imports, the symbol of a nation which, as Uzlar-Pietri says, is "progressively castrating itself." Harbors for exports aren't needed, because hardly anything but oil leaves the country, and the companies do their own harbor work.

Minister Egaña would spend $600 million for great

permanent "Roman" roads, to carry four lanes of traffic and loads as heavy as 100 tons, to be bordered by stately avenues of noble trees, and to run through the mountains, the llanos, the deserts and the selvas even to the jungle border with Brazil. These roads would cost $120,000 a mile, or more than twice what the oil companies spend on theirs. Such a one is being built now, to connect the capital with its seaport and airport. It is the government's proud claim that it will be possible to get to the Caribbean from Caracas in 15 minutes (handy for outgoing Presidents).

Irrigation is badly needed in a country which is semi-arid, but who would benefit, the latifundistas or the conuqueros? Egaña does not specify. Electrification would be nice, too. But peasants who can't afford kerosene for their lamps will hardly be good customers. The irrigation-electrification schemes would be essential in a program of agrarian reform, but that unfortunately is not contained in Minister Egaña's plans.

Actually, more than $100 million a year is being spent on public works, much of it essential upkeep, some of it solid addition to the nation's wealth, some of it mere grandiose display. Barcelona has no sewage system, but its airport is better than Philadelphia's. In the capital the children of the bureaucracy attend the splendid "Republic of Uruguay" school; the bureaucrats themselves have the magnificent University hospital. But there is no public telephone system in eastern Venezuela (the oil companies of course have their private system), and it takes three or four days to journey by bus from Caracas to Maracaibo, 500 kilometers away. Roman temples are reared in a land of primitive huts; the promise of attractive workers' housing in Caracas is just another lure depopulating the rural valleys in the Andes.

"Sowing the petroleum" means, in effect, that a good part of the oil income is siphoned by direct subsidy to plantation owners so that they may continue their exports, and to manufacturers to build up domestic industries. These factories turn out mainly consumers' goods—beer, cigarettes, clothing, liquor, soap, cement, soft drinks, tires, and so on. One and all they are parasitic. Bereft of government subsidies and high tariff protection, they would collapse like a house of cards.

Real planning to rebuild Venezuela's agriculture, and whatever industry is appropriate, is politically impossible now. Such planning requires breaking the power of the latifundistas, the first step to agrarian reform. But the final power is exercised not in the Presidential Palace, or the Capitol, or even in the swank clubs of the plantation owners and cockroach capitalists. The fate of Venezuela is determined at 30 Rockefeller Plaza, the head office of Standard of Jersey. But on its board of directors sit no representatives of Venezuela. The economic life of the country can be paralyzed by a simple motion in Standard's board—a motion, for instance, that Venezuelan oil production be curtailed 25 percent, or 50 percent, in favor of Arabian production. In that decision, Venezuela would have no voice, even though the nation's rickety economy and the revenues of the government would be at stake.

This is the essence of imperialism, its negation of national sovereignty, its mockery of the hopes and decisions of a people. Within the country reigns an *imperium in imperio*—the oil companies with their own private cities and towns, their own private roads and telephone systems, their private ports, their private police. Over both this enclave within a nation, and the nation itself, rules a small group of financial oligarchs in faraway Manhattan.

Impotence marks all of Venezuela's varying governments as mere care-takers, assuring stability so that the wells may pump and the tankers may move their cargoes out to the safe havens of nearby Dutch Aruba and Curaçao. Therefore the air of futility underlying the jeremiads of Venezuela's savants, the irresponsibility and effervescence of its leaders, the dull complacency of its bureaucrats.

Venezuela's lack of real sovereignty is coupled with lack of experience with democratic forms. When the Tyrant Gomez died in 1935, the country awoke to a springtime of comparative liberty after a generation of bizarre cruelty. For the first time in the nation's history, unions of workers and peasants grew, despite periods of repression. Political parties began to develop. Under President Medina, in the early 1940's, it was said that for once there were neither political prisoners nor exiles.

Acción Democrática, with the help of young Army officers, seized power in 1945. This party represented the hopes of the new Venezuela and flourished as a reflex of Roosevelt's New Deal. Under it, the unions grew to be a decisive factor in politics. The leaders of AD tried the Rooseveltian formula of uniting progressive capitalists, such as they were, and the intellectuals with the unions and peasants in a regime of "social peace" supported by the Communists. A section of the Communists revolted against such "Browderism" and formed the group known later as the "black" Communists, from the color of their ballots in the 1947 election. They denounced AD for betraying agrarian reform, for its illusions of cooperation with the oil corporations and Nelson Rockefeller, appropriately or ironically the State Department's expert on Latin America.

AD itself fell in 1948, betrayed by the very Army officers which had helped it to power. "Carlito" Chalbaud, protégé of President Gallegos, so close to the AD leader that he lived in the President's home, organized the *coup d'état*; in deference to the close relationship, Carlito saw to it that the President was escorted safely out of the country. Perhaps the one gain of bloody Gomez's reign of terror had been that he had whipped down the military chieftains and broken their power in favor of his own unitary rule. AD called the army back into politics, and fell by its own stratagem.

President Gallegos, in exile, charged that the oil corporations worked with the army in overthrowing his progressive regime. The truth seems to lie to either side of that claim. The oil companies, like the State Department, desire stability in Latin American governments, and had no basic grievance against AD, even though the growing pressure of the unions was annoying. In Venezuela, the corporations do not care to be aligned too closely with any government, for sure as shooting its days are numbered—at any rate they always have been. The Junta, in denying that it is a tool of the oil companies, can point to its continued efforts to get a better deal on oil royalties. In any event, it bargains sharply for its reward in keeping the lid on Venezuela.

The army denies, too, that it is reactionary. If it had to break the Confederation of Labor and the Oil Workers Federation, it was only because they backed AD to the point of trying to force a *coup d'état* through general strikes, and not because the regime hates unions. The Junta—in a paraphrase of Taft-Hartley—explains that it is not against unions "as such," but resents their political activities. Unions not tied in with AD and the "red" Communists are still legal, but have become anemic under police surveillance. The Junta has not altered the progressive Labor Law or Social Security Law; but in practice the absence of militant unions has weakened the enforcement of both laws and prevented any improvement in them.

It is an anomaly of the current dictatorship that the more uncompromising Communists are still tolerated. At noonday on the busy streets of Caracas, copies of Unión Soviética, the official Soviet magazine, are hawked with stentorian cries. The Soviet-Venezuelan cultural society is active. The *Caracas Journal,* American weekly, in defiance of a ban on foreigners' acting in domestic politics, calls stridently for the suppression of the "black" Communists. The regime's attitude is that only AD and its supporters are under the ban, and certainly the "black" Communists never supported Gallegos, "social peace," or the political strikes which sought to overthrow the Junta in 1949 and 1950.

In Caracas, they say the Junta is not a "dicta*dura*" but a "dicta*blanda*," a play on the Spanish words for "hard" and "soft." Certainly it does not indulge in the bloody orgies of the neighboring Colombian dictatorship. A score of AD and "red" Communists are immured in the Model Prison and others are in exile, but there are no reports of torture. The "legal" unions have a little leeway—but not much since strikes are forbidden. The press censors itself, for the most part. It may be that the rulers of Venezuela have learned from Standard Oil the art of keeping people in chains that do not cut as they bind. The techniques applied to the creation and maintenance of company unions in Bayonne and Baytown come in handy in Venezuela, for a suave business-like government.

Something of this bland spirit is evident in the Junta's recent announcement that free and fair elections will be held in 1952 in which all parties may compete—except Acción Democrática, which polled 75 percent of the votes in the only really free election Venezuela has ever had, and the "red" Communists.

The Junta has declined, so far, to blood any of its troops in Korea, despite State Department pressure. Instead, it dispatched $100,000 in medical supplies. Venezuela, after all, is also a small nation, and reports of the obliteration of the Korean people make sour reading in Latin America. The newsreels of American bombers, likely to make some North Americans boastful of their power, are more apt in Venezuela to stir sympathy with the bombed. In any event, the Junta has troubles enough of its own with feuding army factions and an unstable political situation. It does not care to add to them.

For the visible future Venezuela seems likely to remain the El Dorado of Standard Oil and Shell, with a small minority of Venezuelans invited to share in the Feast of Belshazzar. Unhappily for its own good, this pearl of great price is indefensible. If a Caracas government ever should prove as unregenerate as the current Iranian regime, the state of Zulia surrounding Lake Maracaibo could readily be detached, à la Panama, from the rest of the country and erected into a separate sovereignty under surveillance of the Marines. While the British must land paratroopers in Cyprus, still a thousand miles away, to threaten the Iranian government, our own airborne troops could be in Maracaibo practically overnight. Only a wretched road over the Andes links Maracaibo to the rest of Venezuela.

Even more important, Venezuela lacks Iran's good fortune in having the neighboring Soviet government as a counterpoise in its bargaining.

So close to its imperial masters, the country finds even its politics reflecting the current fashions in Washington. While Roosevelt was in the White House, Acción Democrática pursued a New Deal policy in Caracas. Now that the monopolies run Washington by direct instead of remote control, a pallid Military Junta marks time in Venezuela. It is significant however that an openly reactionary regime can find no foothold at the present time.

Most people there see no allure in capitalism. None of the varicolored parties boost the virtues of free enterprise, dog-eat-dog, and the atomic bomb. Although repression has blocked the development of a socialist solution of the nation's problems, the workers, peasants, and intellectuals are innately socialist.

Picasso's peace dove adorns the University of Caracas student paper.

All Venezuela is watching intently the drama of dying imperialism in Iran. The government hopes that nationalization will choke Iranian production, thereby raising the importance of Venezuelan oil in the world market. Only a few months ago Venezuela for the first time exchanged diplomatic representation with Iran, expressing in veiled terms the hope that both countries could cooperate in bargaining with the international Standard Oil-Shell monopoly.

As for the oil workers, they view Iran as a symbol of hope. Most of the oil unions favor nationalization, but under the Acción Democrática regime such sentiments were submerged in deference to "social peace"; now that the unions are fighting for their very existence, nationalization is more a dream than a specific point in a union program. With the examples of Mexico and Iran before them, it can be expected that nationalization will come more to the front as a demand. That, however, will be within the framework of a popular government whose other fundamental project will be the collectivizing of agriculture.

# BRAZIL, A CHRISTIAN COUNTRY

## BY FRANCISCO JULIAO

From Morro da Queimada, from this Villa Rica de Ouro Preto, the heart of Minas Gerais, which is the portrait and synthesis of Brazil's misery, I write to you fellow citizen and companion, to you living in the fields and in the cities, waiting for the hour of your redemption, and I am sure that you will listen to me, because I am not any longer a voice lost in the vastness of our country.

From all the corners of huge Brazil, from the landless campesino of Parana to the "canoero" of the Amazonas, from the soldier to the general, from the worker of Volta Redonda to the manufacturer of Sao Paulo, from the student of Goiaz to the professor of Guanabara, from the "candango" of Brasilia to the "maloqueiro" of Porto Alegre, from the official to the small grocer, from physicians, lawyers, engineers, Catholics, Protestants, spiritists, Communists and non-Communists, from men of every political party and every philosophical creed I have received hundreds and hundreds of letters and telegrams offering warm support to the Ligas Campesinas (Peasant Leagues) and the struggle we are fighting against the latifundia and for land reform.

From other countries, such as Chile, Uruguay, Peru, Venezuela, and Bolivia, to name a few, I have received calls and invitations. What does all this mean? It means that the people of my country and the brotherly peoples of other countries, the humble and the patriotic, feel that I am the bearer of a high and generous message for the oppressed and the exploited of the cities and the fields, so high and generous that the mercenary

Francisco Juliao is the head of the Peasant Leagues of Brazil, a relatively new organization of poor peasants with a program of agrarian reform much like that which inspired the victory of the Cuban Revolution. The article itself is a speech made at a public meeting of the Peasant Leagues in Ouro Preto and is here presented in a translation made by Uruguayan friends from the text as published in Spanish in the Montevideo weekly *Marcha* of May 18, 1962.

press which serves reaction, the landlords and the trusts, cannot tarnish it with the drivel of its calumnies, base acts, and hatred.

Let us think of Brazil. The picture I am going to paint for you, fellow citizen and companion, is without exaggeration still darker in the rest of the Latin American countries, all of them (with the sole exception of Cuba) dominated by "Christian democracy."

Our population is seventy million. Keep that in mind, we are the fifth country in the world in territorial size and the eighth in population, and you will see what we are reduced to. Let us start with elections because through them we choose the government and the parliament. Both government and parliament with lower case type. Do you know, friend, that less than one fifth of our population voted in the last elections, even though they were the most disputed elections in all our Republic's life? Why is that so? Because illiterates do not vote in a country that is not ashamed to show 90 percent illiteracy among the rural masses and 70 percent in the total population. And those who vote, under what conditions do they go to the polls? That very small percentage of voters, from which privates and sailors are excluded, has not even the right to select its candidates. They do not emerge from the people but are the product of a shady deal, a deal between persons and groups that act according to their own interests. Those groups are the political parties. When, exceptionally, the candidate comes from the masses, he is screened by the parties, he must submit to their requirements, hide his own ideals, twist his conscience, lie to the people. Once he is elected he discards the platform he used during his campaign because he is a prisoner of the array of forces and vested interests that form those groups. Because behind those parties, the big parties, pulling the strings, are the forces that hold economic power.

What are those forces? The landlords, the big manufacturers, the bankers, the go-between bourgeoisie, and above them all, North American imperialism. Those are just the forces that decide in parliament, where the law is made. Their law. If our constitution denies the vote to the illiterate, the sailor, and the soldier, if the electoral system provides unequal treatment for parties and candidates, if the purchasing of votes, the stealing of consciences, the control of propaganda, the counterfeiting of the popular will, and widespread corruption are allowed, what are the results? The landless campesinos, that is, those who form the great majority of our population, are not represented either in the government or in Congress. Whence there occurs, in Brazil and the other representative democracies of Latin America, this curious, grotesque, disgusting, cynical, phenomenon: the landlord makes the law for the campesino, the banker makes the law for the housewife, the shark for the student, the general for the soldier, and imperialism makes the law for our country, the country that it plunders without mercy, as it does in Amapá with the manganese, and through the 400 companies that suck abroad the blood, the sweat, and the tears of millions of Brazilians. With this system, a mixture of tricks and collusion, they construct, build up, balance, maintain, praise, and exalt representative democracy, the more Christian for its being "Western."

You will see now, my brother, my friend, my fellow, some tragic figures, cruel, frightening figures that our representative democracy offers "Christianly" to the world, while other peoples, already liberated from that plague, that lie, that crime, that punishment, that infamy, build a new society, a new civilization, another humanity, without lies or fears, with the land, the factories, the schools, the culture, the bread, the houses, freedom, and the future within reach, if not yet of all, of the great majority.

No less than 80 percent of arable and pasture lands of our country belong to 2 percent of the Brazilians. I am speaking of the best lands, of those that have communications and roads to the great centers of population. There are landowners with more than 200,000 hectares while tens of thousands of campesinos do not own a single inch of land. Those brothers of ours will be buried alive before long, as if planted, and only then will they occupy their seven feet of earth.

Of those arable and pasture lands, less than 10 percent are cultivated. Some people say that if all the plantations of coffee, sugar cane, yerba, millet, cotton, rice, wheat, and other products cultivated in the country were put together, they would not cover the area of the State of Piaui. Stretching from Sergipe to Ceará, the Northeast has a humid strip of about 46,000 kilometers. Of that strip only 4,000 kilometers are occupied by cane and other crops. The rest is idle or under-utilized, subject to real estate speculation or serving as collateral for the big juicy loans that the Banco de Brazil and other credit institutions grant to the landlords. That happens in a zone where the population density is higher than in many European countries and where misery borders despair. That is why the Ligas Campesinas have been born in the Northeast and in the humid strip. But not only in the Northeast is there misery. It is all over the country. Feudal relations prevail everywhere. In the State of Sao Paulo there are 1,400,000 campesinos without land. According to that State, that has enacted an agrarian reform plan considered the most advanced in the country—so advanced that its author, Agriculture Secretary José Bonifacio, has made of it the main plank in his Congressional candidacy's platform—it would take 2,000 years to give land to all those campesinos. In the "mining triangle," it is common to hear the poor campesino say that his 10-year-old child has never tasted cow meat. In Rio Grande Do Sul, the "colono" gives away half of his rice crop as payment for the rent of the land. The civil code defends sharecropping with teeth and nails and consecrates every kind of unrighteousness. Our civil legislation is seriously sick. And old. And the Brazilian still more sick. He is sad. Anciolostomiasis, according to information obtained by Franklin de Oliveira, affects 23 million Brazilians, endemic bocium 18.5 million, paludism 8 million, esquisostomosis 4 million, trachoma one million, syphilis 600,000, leprosy 64,000, and mental diseases 43,000. No less than 100,000 persons die every year of tuberculosis.

Every 42 seconds a child dies, that is 85 every hour, 2,040 every day. Every year, 6 million Brazilians aged under 16 are taken to the cemetery. Of each 1000 children, 350 and even 400 die before reaching one year of age. The average life expectancy in the Northeast is 27 years. More than 30 million Brazilians do not wear shoes, hundreds of thousands live nude, in infested huts, like animals. More than 90 percent of the prostitutes in Brazil are from the country and illiterate. They grow up like flowers over the latifundium's decay. The worker also comes from the fields. And the soldier. All are branded by servitude. All are running away from the big stick, the "capanga," from injustice. But latifundium comes to the cities too, in the soul of the captain of industry, who carries feudalism to the factories. In Brazil every manufacturer is a big landlord. And as the landlord commands more power than the manufacturer because he has lived here longer, something shocking happens: the indifference, the wonderment, or the resistance of the manufacturer to the agrarian reform, notwithstanding that this is the way to create a strong internal market that could liberate him from external pressure. He prefers to be quietly swallowed up by imperialism as the onza does with the yacaré, or give it the lion's share, fearing that an alliance with the underdog could put an end to private property in the land and in the means of production and lead to socialism. That is why they prefer the "Alliance for Progress."

Do you know, my friend and fellow, that only half of the infant population of the country—8 million children—goes to school and that only one tenth of them finishes the primary course? And that education reaches only 950,000 of the 14 million persons between seven and eighteen years old? And last, that only 5 percent of Brazilian youth is able to enter the University?

I could tell you now about the fabulous earnings of that privileged minority that once killed Felipe dos Santos and hung Tiradentes, coming now all together to Ouro Preto, to shed crocodile tears. I prefer to tell you about another mass of oppressed people almost as insecure and exploited as the city or the field workers: the great masses of the middle class without the right to a roof that also demand urgently an agrarian reform. They are the families' heads and housewives haunted by high prices that go up an average of 3.5 percent per month, by the difficulties in the way of educating, caring for, and guiding the family towards a future of decency and security. They are the small storekeepers, small manufacturers, and artisans that are bled white by taxes and by the sharks from within and without.

This is a pale picture of the present Brazil. This is the homeland over which the Southern Cross, so often invoked, shines quietly every night, as it did before the first plunderer arrived, and as it will after we drive out the robbers of its resources.

The democracy we want for Brazil is very different. The name matters very little, as long as it is for the people. Let it be called Christian, popular, or socialist, as long as it brings as its first step a radical agrarian reform. But, I ask you, my fellow and my friend, if it is possible to bring forth such a reform inside the present system. The whole nation knows that a new farce is in the making. The industry of anti-Communism is already at work with enormous publicity. To sustain it, a little safety-box with billions in it is built up, then an alliance of the small minority of the big against the big majority of the small is made, the sacred family unites, the public relations men make dupes of the masses, the most highfalutin slogans are flown to the winds, rivers of money flow, the nation is stirred, and finally the mountain gives birth to a mouse. The comedy is staged again. The magician changes his style, his gestures, his words, but the wand that once belonged to Portuguese colonialism is today in the hands of Uncle Sam. Pan Americanism, the Good Neighbor, the Monroe Doctrine, the Truman Doctrine, the Marshall Plan, Alliance for Progress, Food for Peace, words, panaceas, patches, everything to hide the unending plundering of riches, the remittance of dividends that goes on and on, all in exchange for loans that do not finance industrialization but are used, in compensation, to indemnify the telephone and power companies, in cold cash, at actual rates of exchange without discounts, with the previous deal made in Washington, between smiles, under the dance of the millions, the applause of the ruling oligarchy, the muffled rebelliousness of the people, and the sell-out of our country. They run to save the Northeast—as if Brazil were now only the Northeast—from hunger and poverty, and also from the "demagoguery of bad Brazilians" interested in harassing the "Christian family," in installing the rule of the "wall," in Cubanizing the country against its "glorious democratic traditions," in installing "foreign" regimes, alien to our peaceful natures. For these last minute "saviors," the "Christian family" is that which lives in a palace, travels in a Cadillac convertible, and owns the land, the cattle, the banks, the industry, the commerce, the public job, and the people's life. The Christian family is not the one who lives in a hut, in the "favela," in the "maloca," in the dead end, or barely subsists in the latifundium, under the violence of share-cropping, the barracks, the body-guard, the police torturer. The Christian family is that of the landlord who arms himself to the teeth throughout the country with the rifle or the machine gun, to parade as a feudal lord the private ownership of the land.

Brazil, a "Christian country," has land to spare, but there is not enough land for millions of campesinos. Brazil, a "Christian country," has inexhaustible resources, but also hundreds of thousands of unemployed. Brazil, a "Christian country," has landlords that live off the rent from one hundred, two hundred, five hundred, one thousand houses, while there are millions crowded in miserable huts like pigs. Brazil, a "Christian country," has millionaires that make a 9000 percent profit on their capital that multiplies as fast as the germs of pest, and, like those murderers, coldly kill those who make possible the miracle of the multiplication. Brazil, a "Christian country," has the sad privilege of having the highest infant mortality rate in Latin America, in spite of the industrialization and the development so much vaunted during the most foreign-dominated administration in the history of Brazil. Brazil, a "Christian country," is underdeveloped, underfed, subjugated. Everything here ends in pillage, lies, theft, insolence. Now agrarian reform is fashionable, the subject of the day, the most important issue in this election year. Then, the young Minister of Agriculture, owner of many acres of land in an area where the campesino is most miserable, runs all over the country showing off this agrarian reform bill, hailing it as the cure-all the system needs. When one peruses the bill, one becomes sure that a Minister in the times of the Portuguese Empire would have drafted a bolder bill and obtained the support even of the slave-owners. Education tenderly cared for by the profitable industry of the private schools, is discussed everywhere, while the number of illiterates goes up and the possibilities diminish for the youth, the son of the worker, or of the middle class, to go to school or even to dream of college. Wages, swallowed up by inflation, provide no longer for daily bread, which is not ours any more but belongs to the wheat trust. Freedom in this "Christian country" means not to touch the privileges of the ruling caste. Human dignity in this "Christian country" is measured by the bank account, the factory chimneys, the big jobs, and the genuflexions before Mr. Kennedy.

I confess to you, brother, friend, and fellow, that I would pray, and with me millions of Brazilians, a Lord's prayer for the eternal rest of this democracy that fattens the shark and starves the people, grants tax-exemptions to the landlords and denies the land to the campesino, allows a corporation to make a 9000 percent profit but orders a machine gun pointed at the chest of the worker who strikes for a wage raise, gives foreign investment a free hand to monopolize the country's resources and moreover lets it freely transfer its earnings abroad, manufactures field marshals, five-star generals and admirals, but denies stability to the sergeant and the vote to the soldier and the sailor. The law is enforced only when it favors the powerful, that is to say "the Christian family," and so much so that social welfare is blackmail, rural unions still do not exist, the robber of the poor does not go to jail, and not a single provision of labor legislation is ever made to operate to favor the campesino. The Communist Party is denied the right to put up its own candidates for public office—and this does not happen even in Catholic Italy, the Italy of that kind and friendly "campesino" Juan XXIII—without any justification, as the party exists anyway, publishes its press, takes part in the political life of the country, and makes alliances with other parties.

I do not believe that the redemption of my country will come from ballots. Or from elites. Or from the Christian family. It will come, and this I do believe, from the desperate masses, the landless campesino, the idle unemployed or underpaid worker, from the student without college, from the children without future, from the old people without past, from the illiterate, from the soldier and sailor without vote, from the poor father, from the priest who does not give his blessing to Uncle Sam, from the intellectual who does not hire out his pen or sell his conscience, from the artisan, from the small storekeeper, from the housewife, from all those who have a heart to feel and a mouth to sing the words of our national anthem: "Let our fatherland be free or let us die for Brazil."

# ANDES AND SIERRA MAESTRA

## BY SEBASTIAN SALAZAR BONDY

"A little news item from Lima, Peru, tells a potentially big story," begins an editorial in the *New York Times* of November 15th. "It is about Indian peasants—8,000 of them—in the old Inca capital of Cuzco, high in the Andes, clashing with the police." The following article tells what is behind that little news item. The author is one of Peru's outstanding writers, having twice received the National Prize of the Theater of Peru (1947 and 1951) and once the National Prize of Journalism. In 1961, he was awarded the Leon de Greiff Hispanic-American Poetry Prize in Caracas, Venezuela. He is co-director of the weekly *Libertad,* organ of the Peruvian Social-Progressive movement.—The Editors

Foreign observers tend to conclude, after visiting Peru, that a second revolutionary front could appear very soon in our country. We Peruvians, however, are less optimistic, not because we think the situation here is more stable than in other nations of Latin America, but because the maturing of the subjective conditions for such a revolt lags behind the evident crisis in objective conditions. The socio-economic abyss becomes greater and greater, imperialistic penetration deeper, misery more extensive, and the accumulation of wealth by the oligarchical caste more and more rapacious. Yet, on the other hand, the isolation of the nation, the "denationalization" of the masses, the repressive measures of the police, etc., also operate efficiently in preventing the formation of a clear popular consciousness and the consolidation of a revolutionary will-power. Nevertheless, whatever the delays, the zero hour will come. Many signs announce that a tiny spark can set the Andes ablaze, and though some sporadic flames have burned out quickly, reality shows that the embers are still there.

## For Each Peruvian a Ration of Hunger

It is impossible to speak of the foreseeable Peruvian Revolution without sketching, however summarily, the economic and social picture of Peru. The overall statistics are pathetic, more pathetic than the most eloquent words. Of 11 million inhabitants (according to official data of the 1961 Census), 13 percent or one sixth of the total, monopolizes half of the national income. The peasantry especially, (56 percent of the population) receives only 13 percent of the national income. Cultivable land is very scarce, and in addition is controlled by a few: 1.5 percent owns 63 percent of the richest agricultural soil. The rest belongs to the Indians (the *ayllus* of pre-Columbian origin) and to small landowners. Large agricultural enterprises, in the hands of native and foreign landlords (such as Grace & Co.), are oriented toward cultivation for export, thus reducing the quantity available for domestic consumption. Furthermore a periodic increase in prices manifestly tends to depress sales. *Latifundism* is integrated with banking, mining, and import interests, which control the foreign exchange market and credit (the interest rate is one of the highest in the world, at times reaching as much as 22 percent.) If to this one adds that the production of energy (petroleum, electricity, coal) is monopolized by North American enterprises and that new investment avoids industry and instead flows into speculative and wasteful channels, (urban property and housing, luxury imports, etc.), the picture becomes even darker.

The peasant is the ultimate victim of the entire system. He is exploited by the landlord, the mining companies, the businessmen, even the state; all of whom gain in the long run from his low level of living. The city worker, though also exploited and despite his low wages, seems privileged in comparison to his country cousin. The Quechua Indian is not even touched by the few social laws, the possibility of individual advancement, education, or any other minimal advantage enjoyed by the worker in a capitalistic society. The nutritional content of the Peruvian's diet is among the world's worst—he consumes about 2,000 calories and about 20 grams of proteins daily, according to information from the FAO. These are averages; and since the favored segments of the population obviously have a much better diet, it follows that the farmer and the worker consume even less than these low figures would suggest—probably no more than a third of what the experts say is needed for an adequate diet. The picture is even more sordid if one looks at the level of sanitation (only 20 percent of cities and towns have water and sewage systems), or the level of education (each year 800,000 children are left without schools, and 60 percent is a conservative estimate of the national illiteracy rate), or the level of housing (9 million Peruvians are badly or dreadfully sheltered).

The economic and social structures have their logical political counterpart. Landlords, bankers, and importers are integrated with the managers and agents of the imperialist companies into a colonial caste which has controlled the country since independence. This caste has built up a politico-judicial structure which is democratic in appearance but definitely dictatorial in nature. In addition to monopolizing the formal positions of power, the caste also controls the parties of the Right and Center, the large and medium-sized press, and other means of expression. For the economic domination of the state, they have invented two unusual agencies: one is the so-called Registry of Deposits and Consignments (*Caja de Depósitos y Consignaciones*), an enterprise formed jointly by the six largest banks, which has charge of collecting taxes. Subsequently, after deduction of generous commissions, these are deposited in those same six private credit enterprises, which thus operate with and profit from the people's money. The other *ad hoc* institution is the Central Reserve Bank (*Banco Central de Reserva*), a bank of issue the management of which consists of representatives of the private banks—tightly associated with local and outside monopolies—and delegates from the executive branch of the government. Since the executive power emanates not from the popular will, as formality would have one believe, but from previous elections manipulated by the dominant economic interests—be it by compromising candidates through contracts and loans or through various kinds of fraud—the will of the houses of finance prevails over that of the many.

Evils tend to aggravate themselves. The population, increasing at the rate of 3.5 percent a year, will reach 25 million by 1981. Quite apart from the probable depopulation of agricultural zones, this demographic flood will greatly increase all the problems to which we have already referred. Nothing indicates that economic growth (despite the Alliance for Progress and other stories of the same kind) will proceed at a greater or similar speed. At the last Punta del Este Conference, it was stated that the fundamental objective of the Alliance for Progress was to reach an annual growth-rate of 2.5 percent in the gross national product per person. Allowing for the rate of growth of the Latin American population (3 percent), this would mean an overall increase of GNP of 5.5 percent. The Peruvian figure for 1961 was a bit more than 3 percent. This was more than absorbed by the increase in population: there was no progress but rather recession. And we continue and will continue to retrogress. Each Peruvian comes into the world with a ration—each year larger—of hunger. And the peasant is the one who receives the largest share in this distribution of want and misery.

## The War for the Reconquest of the Communities

Perhaps this is why the peasants are assigned a decisive role in the Peruvian Revolution. That vast mass of men and women—the majority of which speaks no Spanish—is illiterate and exists outside the electoral structure, patiently nursing a most ancient hatred. It is apparently passive, without aspirations, almost beastly, in the shallow judgment of the comfortable city dweller, racist in his Hispanism and consequent Westernism. Many times torn from the land and the cattle, his traditional occupations, the Indian goes to work in the mines, in search of better pay, and there ends his days with tuberculosis. Or he emigrates, for the same reason, to the city, where he builds his precarious hut of mats and adobe in the circle of *barriadas* (illegal areas), which surround the principal urban nuclei of Peru. In the hacienda as peon, in the Andean heights as *comunero* (communal tenant owner), in the pit as laborer, in the city as outcast—everywhere the Indian shows his distrusting presence. The professional politician shuns him, for his voteless opinion counts for nothing in the democratic farce. The Left strives with difficulty to gain his friendship, which is hard to conquer due to previous and frequent betrayals. The army, thanks to compulsory military service, manages to impress upon the drafted Indian the form and manner of military life but never turns him into an individual assimilated into the rest of the national community. The Church, also failing to bring about his social integration, adds Catholic superstition to his inherited world of magic. A long time ago it was established that the so-called "Indian problem" is not one of educational, hygienic, or technical preparation, for the most commonplace schooling will give him perfectly useless knowledge. To one who lives in such misery, soap is exotic or superfluous, and agricultural education means nothing to a mere slave on an estate. The problem is economic above all else, and only a real agrarian reform—not the demagogic make-believe kind of Peru, Venezuela, or Colombia, which furthers the interests of the oligarchies while deceiving their Yankee partner—can prepare the awakening of the Indian people from a long sleep.

It is precisely economic factors which have caused in recent times an unprecedented collective action by the old Quechua communities. Seeing this, the plutocracy, with a McCarthy-type vocabulary, has raised its voice to the skies about undefined fidelista and Communist agitation. In fact, the so-called "invasions" of private haciendas by Indian farmers have been a spontaneous liberation movement, the further development of which can bring an insurrectional tide of a new kind to the Americas.

For example, the Indian community or *ayllu* of Yerus Yacán lived for four centuries—without counting those preceeding the Spanish conquest—on a wide territory in the Province of Pasco in the Andean center of Peru. In 1619, an officer of the Spanish Crown demarcated the property of this community and gave it corresponding legal recognition. In the first decade of this century there appeared in the zone a North American enterprise, the Cerro de Pasco Corporation, which bought, with a view to mineral exploitation, the Hacienda Paria (up to then belonging to a religious community) neighboring on Yerus Yacán. The signed document between the Yankee company and the Convent of the Nazarenes took great care not to define the borderline between the hacienda acquired by Cerro de Pasco and the Indian community. The wire fences built immediately after the transaction shrank the adjacent area considerably. It was in the middle of 1960 that the plunder became impudent: caretakers of the Cerro de Pasco Corporation forced shepherds to abandon their traditional lands. These shepherds were unarmed and gave way to pressure, clearly remembering that in the previous year the same foreign company, aided by the police, had massacred members of the community of Rancas in a similar situation. Yerus Yacán presented before the courts an interdict for recovery. This mattered little to the Yankees, however, for the tribunals, as they knew from experience, have their price. While delaying judicial action, agents were sent out to burn pastures and destroy huts, each time penetrating further into the communal property. In an assembly of the entire community its leaders were then authorized to advance peacefully, so as to reconquer lost properties as far as the line indicated by the 1619 document. The Cerro de Pasco Corporation and the Association of Central Breeders of Wool-bearing Animals (*Associación de Criadores de Lanares del Centro*)—a regional organization of latifundists—denounced this "armed invasion" before the government and called it the start of a Cuban-style revolution. The government sent out assault troops, and, after a waiting period to give time for an alarmed public opinion to subside, attacked the defenseless Indians and threw them off their land after beating, harassing, and in some cases killing them. However, after the first days, the Indians reacted and returned to the same lands. Then the courts of Lima took up the case, though now, ten months later, they have yet to resolve the dispute.

This case is not exceptional. Similar actions have taken place in the same region (Pasco) and in the North and South of Peru. In order to carry them out, the *comuneros* have a kind of special commando, generally made up of those among them who have had military training. They use military tactics, but are unarmed and non-violent. From time to time, the Lima newspapers publish stories about such and such a community's having "invaded" properties of latifundists or miners. The informed reader knows what is happening. Disgusted with being dispossessed, lacking official justice, the Indians have decided to take through their own effort what has always belonged to them. A justice-seeking movement is awakening.

Why?

Different factors contribute, though often not the work of professional political agitators, so blamed by those who are concerned to obscure the real issues. The *comuneros* lack any articulate political thought and do not want a revolution. They are moved by a thwarted sense of justice, by a desire to recover a possession, the land, which for them is endowed with a divine nature, the *Pachamama* worshiped by the Incas, which is the same principle venerated by all agrarian peoples. In the face of the weak support lent by the Left press to their efforts for recovery, the Indians have showed themselves wary, trusting more in the friendly (or seemingly so) elements of authority than in the doctrinaire adhesion of revolutionary parties.

Taking account of this experience, the Communists, the Social-progressives, and others of Left tendency in Peru are now placing special emphasis on attracting the rebel *comuneros* to their cause and on adding to their rebelliousness a socialistic consciousness. Up to now, however, the atomized Peruvian Left has not succeeded in devising an effective strategy. Apart from one faction of Trotskyites, they have all attempted to play the electoral game. The uselessness of this was demonstrated in the recent frustrated elections which showed that the Left cannot compete in publicity, campaign machinery, etc., with the parties of the Right and Center, supported as they are by the financial largesse of the oligarchy. The Trotskyite faction referred to began a year ago to follow an adventurist revolutionary tactic, holding up banks to acquire funds to aid peasant uprisings and organizing a still-tiny and as yet untested band of guerrillas in a narrow valley in the Province of Cuzco. This approach does not seem feasible either, both because the organizers lack the indispensable means (leaders, arms, bases, etc.) and because the peasant mass has yet to react favorably to the political call.

Basic work, it would seem, must be directed to the formation among the popular masses, especially the Indians, of a political consciousness. Unfortunately, little can be expected of the trade unions which are run by strike-breakers, bureaucrats, or petty politicians—witness the General Confederation of Peruvian Workers (*Confederación General de Trabajadores del*

*Perú*) controlled by the social-traitors of APRA. One must start
with the mood of the *comuneros* in the agricultural regions of
the Andes where, besides ancient traditions of a hegemony lost
through Spanish conquest, there is the picture of economic
squalor sketched in the statistics already cited.

### The Fire Will Descend from the Andes
The problem is, above all, one which must be solved from
within. The 7 million Indians and mestizos possess a culture—
in the sense of modern anthropology—however much it may
have been defensively pressed into Western molds. The study
of this culture is indispensable—this closed universe perceived
by Peruvians of the coast and cities only in folk art, in folk
poetry with its simplicity and beauty, in dance and song; or
perceived by academic scholarship abstractly and idealistically,
through studies of such institutions as the *ayllu* or community,
and the *servicacuy* or trial marriage. It is impossible to turn the
Indian into a revolutionary through mere political agitation.
We must find and understand the spirit of Quechua man. It
is useless and silly to ask him to use our language, our rational
system, our cultural and intellectual complex, while not asking
of ourselves the inverse process. The case of Peru is very different
from that of Cuba. The Cuban peasant—like the Venezuelan,
Argentine, Brazilian, and many another—may have been little
more than a slave, yet between him and the intellectual there
was a common ground: language, nationality, history. Martí,
symbol of Independence, was as much in the heart of the
*guajiro* as in the student's far away in Havana or Santiago.
In Peru, on the contrary, though the student be a nonconformist
and in favor of a peasant rebellion, there are abysmal differences between him and the Indian: language separates them,
the glorious history of one tells the story of the oppression of
the other. They belong to distinct nations, whether one likes
it or not. The concept of integration between the two groups—
Indian and white—has to be conceived of as a dynamic search
of the latter for the former, and not inversely.
It is obvious that there is never going to be an effective
program of reform coming from the wielders of economic power,
nor from the agents of an imperialism which exploits alike the

nation's riches and its human beings, snatching from them their age-old property, throwing them into the mines to die, turning them into servants, peons, miserably paid laborers shorn of all legal rights. The establishment of the oligarchy exhausts its powers in creating a social security system according to a law which, as they used to say in colonial times, "is respected but not complied with." A long time ago, when they were still militant revolutionaries, the Apristas coined an expression: "Half-breeds cheap, sugar dear." (*Cholo barato, azucar caro.*) There in a nutshell is the formula which has been used to keep 56 percent of the Peruvian population in subhuman conditions. Now there is only one way that the sugar—or the cotton or the petroleum, the story is the same—can confer its benefits on the whole country. Those millions of "cheap half-breeds" will descend, as Carleton Beals foresaw many years ago, with torches lit in the Andes.

The ballot boxes—"representative democracy" participated in by two out of eleven million Peruvians—are part of the oligarchical farce. No one, not even those who use them, believes in them. But the other way, unless there is an explosion somewhere else on the Continent, requires a preparation which has scarcely yet begun. How long it will take cannot now be foretold, but there can be no doubt of the ultimate outcome however long it may be. The peasants of Peru must act to recover homelands seized from them, just as the *comuneros* of Yerus Yacán acted to recover their lost lands. When that time comes, the Andes will become, as Fidel Castro predicted, "an immense Sierra Maestra."

# REPORT FROM ECUADOR

## BY MANUEL AGUSTIN AGUIRRE

Ecuador has been ruled for a long time by two fundamental oligarchical groups. One, centered in the Ecuadorian sierra is landowning, feudal, and economically backward; the other, based on the coast, is more developed economically owing to its connections with foreign import and export trade. The first group has constituted the principal nucleus of the Conservative Party which also has ramifications known as *Arnismo* and Social-Christianism. The second is somewhat more liberal in character.

It can be stated that what has been taking place in Ecuador is a conflict between oligarchical groups rather than a class struggle. The lack of industrial development has prevented the emergence of an industrial bourgeoisie which could oppose the feudal landlords. There exists only one dominant class of landowners, big merchants, and bankers whose factions continually dispute for control of the government, big business deals, and budgetary privileges.

These coastal and mountain elites have generally expressed themselves through two traditional parties: the Conservative and the Liberal. The former is closely allied to the Catholic Church and exploits by religious as well as economic means. The latter insincerely repeats the bourgeois trilogy "Liberty, Equality, Fraternity," impossible of realization in a semi-feudal, semi-colonial country. Both parties agree in maintaining indefinitely the archaic, backward socio-economic structure of the country. Both ceaselessly seek their own enrichment at the cost of hardships and misery to the Ecuadorian people. Both are tied to North American imperialism.

The awakening of the working masses who yearn for just and immediate improvements, the new ideological currents em-

Dr. Agustin Aguirre is Vice Rector of Central University, Quito.

bodied in the parties of the Left which have appeared on the political scene, and the increasing loss of prestige of the Conservative and Liberal parties were all factors that forced the oligarchies, especially the more conservative one, to adopt a new strategy. This consisted of backing certain individuals who appear to be "independent" and "unaffiliated with any party" but who, because of origin, intellectual training, and unlimited ambition, can be helpful collaborators for the unchanging purpose of misdirecting and deceiving the people and of continuing to dominate and exploit them.

One of these key individuals is Dr. José María Velasco Ibarra, who, for about thirty years, with the exception of short intervals, has played the leading role assigned to him by the Ecuadorian elites. He brought to the part special qualifications: he was a man of conservative background but ambiguous ideology that permitted him to display, like a rainbow, a variety of colors. This political chameleon had, in addition, a talent for popular, facile, and flowing oratory which, combined with an absolute lack of scruples, enabled him to evolve a boundless demagogy and to delude the Ecuadorian people for many, many years.

It was the conservative landowning oligarchy from the sierra that first encouraged and financed Velasco Ibarra; later on, he also obtained the support of the commercial and financial elite of the coast. While he alternated in his efficient service to those who financed him generously with millions drawn from the sweat and blood of the workers, he hurled insults against "rascals and thieves," deceiving with big words and theatrical gestures the politically uneducated masses, who knew that they were the victims of the rascals and thieves but not that these enemies were hiding behind the gestures and words of their supposed redeemer.

Velasco even formed his own elite, giving free rein to his closest adherents. He placed these associates in important posts thus creating a new layer of rich men who constituted his financial reserve. Through a strategy of refined hypocrisy, he did not fill his own pockets as others do, since he wanted to appear "honest and incorruptible." Instead, he put millions into the pockets of his intimate friends who then financed his ostentatious and noisy presidential campaigns. It is hard to find in Latin America a more clamorous and successful case of sham.

In the million-dollar campaign that brought him to power for the fourth time in 1960, he over-did himself as never before in demagogic promises. From his words flowed rivers of milk and honey that were to stream endlessly through the country. Nevertheless, on taking office his first decrees raised indirect taxation that most affected consumers, and enacted legal and monetary reforms which favored the groups wanting to recover their electoral investments. All this was crowned by Decree Number 33, which imposed a monetary devaluation. This meant and still means—for the new government has done nothing to change the situation in this respect—greater privileges for the privileged and greater poverty for the working people of Ecuador.

As a result, the Workers Confederation of Ecuador (CTE) called a national general strike to demand that Congress repeal these emergency laws. The strike was supported by the students and the majority of the people, including *velasquistas* disillusioned by the demagogy of the government. The government answered with mounted police and machine-gun fire. Some workers and students were killed. As more victims fell, mainly high school and university students, the people became incensed.

Velasco made an attempt, with the support of the Army, to proclaim himself dictator. He had done it on other occasions, notably, on March 30th, 1946, when he overthrew the progressive Constitution passed by the Constitutional Assembly of 1944-1945. Nevertheless, this last and most recent bid for absolute power failed and the demagogue was deposed. However, he imprisoned his successor, the Vice President and presiding officer of Congress, Dr. Carlos Julio Arosemena Monroy. Despite this, Arosemena was proclaimed President of the Republic by Congress and finally took office after the withdrawal of Dr. Camilo Gallegos Toledo, head of the Supreme Court, who had been offered the Presidency at the same time by part of the Army.

A few words about the new executive, Dr. Arosemena. He comes from an old established banking family of the coastal city of Guayaquil. His political career began and developed under the wing of Dr. Velasco Ibarra. He directed the latter's last political campaigns and was his running mate in the most recent election which took place June 5th, 1960. During the first months of Dr. Velasco's fourth term, while the latter inundated the country, as usual, with a flood of oratory, Vice President Arosemena was generally silent, avoiding participation in certain official functions. This provoked comments about the estrangement of the two rulers. The discord was accentuated later, when an open quarrel began between a sector of Congress—presided over by Dr. Arosemena—and the chief executive, Dr. Velasco.

An important incident in the persistent differences between Arosemena and Velasco was Arosemena's decision to accept an invitation to visit the Soviet Union. The trip was made against the will of the Council of Ministers which, Arosemena declared, made its objection after he had accepted the invitation. The trip evoked sympathy towards him on the Left despite the fact that on his return from the USSR he said hardly a word about that country. Undoubtedly, this new support helped him get to power through the cruel struggle mentioned above, fought mainly by the Workers Confederation (CTE), the Federation of University Students (FEUE), and the Left political parties.

The new President began by organizing a Cabinet of National Unity that includes representatives of the most reactionary forces of the Right as well as men vaguely identified with the Left. The CTE, the FEUE, and the radical parties (Revolutionary Socialist and Communist) have given the government conditional support, expecting a solid program of popular reform.

The new government of national unity, made up of opposing and contradictory forces, lacks a definite administrative policy. In the near future it will have to define itself by adopting a position to the Right or in the Center or—less probably—of advance to the Left. In the meantime, the government has promised, among other things, agrarian reform. This reform was demanded by a mass meeting of over 20,000 Indian peasants before whom Arosemena promised the abolition of feudal and semi-feudal conditions and fiscal reforms to reduce the indirect taxation that strangles the consuming public and to establish direct measures to tax those who own the country's wealth. In international affairs, the government has spoken for relations with the United States as well as with the USSR, but has done nothing toward the establishment of relations with the latter country. It has also promised to observe the principles of non-intervention and self-determination, but has kept in the foreign ministry a reactionary who is an enemy of the Cuban Revolution.

Actually, as President Arosemena himself has declared, no revolution has taken place here, certainly none in the true sense of the word. What has occurred is an official split, perhaps only a turn of the coin. It seems certain that, as on other occasions, the bloodshed by the people will have been in vain, that there will be a continuation of rule by the dominant oligarchies that alternate in power.

But the working class of the country is acquiring a clear understanding of the present situation and of its destiny. Backed by the peasants and other progressive forces, it will yet make its REVOLUTION, a revolution in capital letters, a socialist revolution like Cuba's, the only revolution that will really liberate the oppressed peoples of Latin America and of the world.

# NOTES ON LATIN AMERICA

BY PAUL M. SWEEZY AND
LEO HUBERMAN

During the last three weeks of January and the first week of February, we visited six Latin American countries (Mexico, Chile, Argentina, Uruguay, Brazil, and Venezuela). We had a very specific objective, to discuss the possibility of a Spanish-language edition of *MR* (see full report next month), as well as the more general objectives of establishing contacts and improving our understanding of Latin American realities. We met and talked, often at great length, with dozens of people, mostly political leaders, economists, sociologists, political scientists, and students in these and other fields. For obvious reasons, it was easier for us to establish relations with people of the Left; and, given the very short time available, we made few efforts to go outside these circles, which in any case are very broad in Latin America and undoubtedly include the best and most stimulating minds. What we were seeking throughout was not to accumulate knowledge of facts—for that purpose four weeks in a good library would have been much more productive—but to get a better "feel" for the situation and to develop a more assured perspective within which to place the facts not only of the past and present but of the future as well.

## What Kind of Revolution?

Since the Cuban Revolution, it has become commonplace to talk about the "Latin American Revolution." Even the most resolute counter-revolutionaries, like those who are now sitting in the seats of power in Washington, join the chorus, assuring us that their fondest wish is to help the Latin Americans achieve their revolution. "We're all socialists now," said the English Liberal politician Sir William Harcourt, as the 19th century drew to a close. In the same way, with regard to Latin America, it seems that we're all revolutionaries now. Under these circumstances, if we are to avoid ambiguity we must say precisely what we mean by the word "revolution."

As used in what follows, "revolution" means two things

which are as indissolubly linked as the two sides of a coin. First, it means the overthrow of the old ruling class (or classes) and the accession to power of a new ruling class (or classes). And second, it means a radical change in property relations. Cuba has already had a revolution in precisely this sense, and the most important questions that can be asked about the other countries of Latin America are whether and when they are going to have their revolutions.

But before we can answer these questions, we must inquire whether more than one kind of revolution, in the sense indicated, is possible in Latin America today. More specifically, do Latin American countries face the choice of bourgeois revolution or socialist revolution? It is widely believed that they do, and we ourselves have been inclined to share the belief at least with respect to some of the countries. We are now convinced, however, not only that this is an error but also that it makes difficult if not impossible any clear thinking about the future course of events in Latin America.

A bourgeois revolution can take place only in a country in which property relations and ruling class are non-bourgeois. In the case of Latin America, those who speak in terms of a possible bourgeois revolution usually have in mind a picture of the kind of society which grew up in colonial days and which survived more or less intact through the 19th century. Whatever one may choose to call societies of this kind, they were certainly not bourgeois in the usual sense of the term, from which it follows that it is quite logical to call a revolutionary transformation of one of them, such as took place in Mexico in the two decades after 1910, a bourgeois revolution. In the rest of Latin America, however, similar transformations have taken place by more evolutionary (though by no means always non-violent) processes, and the societies of today are everywhere very different from those of colonial times. In particular, the traditional landowning aristocracies are now mixed up with the financial, commercial, and manufacturing bourgeoisies. Landowners have invested in towns and cities; merchants and bankers have bought land; families have intermarried. By now it is probably safe to say that in every country the bourgeoisie owns the land as well as the capital. This is not to say that the characteristics of the bourgeoisie, including its social attitudes and mental habits, have not been influenced by its heritage from the past: obviously they have been, and this is a fact of importance to an understanding of the present. What it does mean is that any analysis and, still more, any course of action that is based on the assumption of division and conflict of interest between landlords and capitalists is bound to go wrong. There is only one ruling class in Latin America today, and it is basically bourgeois in its outlook and interests. It follows that the only possible revolution is one that overthrows bourgeois rule and installs the peasantry and/or the proletariat as the new ruling class(es). The other side of the revolutionary coin can only be the substitution of socialist for bourgeois property relations. In other words, *the only possible revolution in Latin America today is a socialist revolution.*

Only if we keep this firmly in mind can we pose the right questions about Latin America. Instead of asking whether there will be a bourgeois revolution, we have to ask what kind of reforms the bourgeoisie which is already in power is capable of making in its own system. And in discussing revolution, we must focus attention on the development of forces with the will and ability to overthrow the bourgeoisie and build socialism. Let us consider these two problems in turn.

## Why Revolution Is Necessary

What may be called the "reform potential" in Latin America of course varies from country to country. Nevertheless, we have no hesitation in saying (1) that in general this potential is low; and (2) that in no country is it high enough to hold out hope of a solution to the increasingly urgent problems of economic development within the framework of the existing system. The reasons for this poor opinion of the Latin American ruling classes' ability to reform their own societies are numerous: here we can only mention the two that seem to us most important.

In the first place, the very fact that the owners of land and the owners of capital are merged together in a single ruling class strongly militates against the carrying out of the kind of thoroughgoing agrarian reforms that are the *sine qua non* of continuing economic development. If the picture of an urban bourgeoisie in conflict with a decadent rural aristocracy were accurate, then there would be real hope of effective land reform within the framework of capitalism. But as we have already seen, this is not the case, and it is very doubtful whether any Latin American bourgeoisie has the will or discipline to impose drastic reforms on itself. This explains, for example, the otherwise baffling fact that Brazil, where industrial development has gone farther and faster in recent years than anywhere else and where an expansion of agricultural production has become a matter of extreme urgency, nevertheless does nothing but talk about agrarian reform.

In the second place, no Latin American country can expect to achieve economic devolopment of a kind that will really benefit the masses of its people unless it also achieves genuine national independence, that is to say, unless it breaks the economic stranglehold that U. S. imperialism now has on the whole area. This, however, the Latin American ruling classes cannot do and even do not want to do. The notion that there is a powerful national bourgeoisie in these countries anxious to break away from U. S. domination and also prepared to go through with it even if it hurts their own interests, is unfortunately a myth. The influence of U. S. capital in the private sector of their economies is pervasive and by no means limited to direct ownership relations (in the world of today control of technology is sometimes even more important than ownership), and the public sector, which is relatively large in some countries, is naturally operated by and for the benefit of the ruling classes. Conflicts of interest between native and foreign capitalists of course do exist, but they are certainly subordinate to the common interest both groups have in exploiting the human and natural resources of the region. And to this powerful tie is added another, common fear of revolution from below. The Latin American bourgeoisies would like to be treated as equals by their North American brothers, but they are not going to jeopardize their wealth and privileges—which, incidentally, are most impressive by anyone's standards—in any quixotic struggles for national independence. But without national independence, the Latin American countries will remain in effect colonial appendages of the North American metropolis. And their most basic and intractable difficulties arise precisely from their past history and present status as colonial appendages.

We have long been convinced that only under socialism

can the countries of Latin America meet the great demographic, technological, and social challenges of the 20th century. What we saw and heard on the spot in the last few weeks has greatly strengthened that conviction. In terms of objective conditions, there can be no doubt that Latin America needs and is ripe for socialist revolution, not at some distant date in the future but right now.

### Are More Revolutions Imminent?

Does this mean that we can expect a rapid spread of revolutionary processes in one or more regions of Central and South America? Many people, including ourselves, have in fact entertained such expectations ever since the victory of the Cuban Revolution four years ago. Unfortunately, we have now come to the reluctant conclusion that this revolutionary optimism was, and still is, based more on wishful thinking than on a sober estimate of possibilities. Our present view is that further successful revolutions are not likely to take place in Latin America in the near future.

The reader is asked to note particularly that we say *successful* revolutions are not likely in the near future. *There is no intention to deny that revolutionary upheavals may take place and may even, as happened in Bolivia in 1952, bring revolutionary regimes to power.* The trouble is that the countries where this could happen in the near future are the weakest and poorest countries, those which lack the human and material resources to build a new social order in the face of the certain hostility of the U. S. on which they are economically dependent and of the ruling classes of their more developed and powerful neighbors. The fate of the Bolivian Revolution tells all too clear a story: it has gradually degenerated and one often hears it said in South America today that the Bolivian government is more under the thumb of the U. S. Embassy than any other government on the continent. In the world of the mid-20th century, it is unfortunately true that successful revolutions can occur only in countries that have already achieved a certain degree of development. And this means, so far as Latin America is concerned, that the pace of revolutionary transformation will be set not by the smaller and weaker countries but by the larger and stronger ones. More concretely, the countries to watch are Brazil, Argentina, Mexico, Chile, Peru, Venezuela. And it is by no means clear that even these more developed countries could sustain revolutions unless several were involved and able to lend each other mutual support. It may quite possibly turn out that the next stage of the Latin American Revolution will involve all or most of the countries in the region.

There are two principal reasons why, in our judgment, this next stage is not imminent. First, the existing regimes in the big Latin American countries, despite all their difficulties and problems, are hardly on the verge of collapse. Some of them have considerable popular support; all dispose over armed forces which (so far at any rate) seem to be reasonably reliable; and all can count on U. S. financial and probably also military backing (if in South Vietnam, why not in South America?). Under these circumstances, only broadly based, well led, and well armed revolutionary movements could hope to seize power. This points to the second reason why successful revolutions are not imminent: such revolutionary movements do not yet exist in Latin America. But rather than attempt further generalizations along these lines, we may perhaps more profitably comment briefly on each of the large countries we visited. We follow the order of our itinerary.

## Mexico

In recent years, Mexico has been the most stable of all the large Latin American countries. The rate of economic growth has been relatively high, and the political system which emerged from the turbulent years of the Revolution has proved to be a remarkably effective instrument of bourgeois rule. (For an excellent description and analysis of these and related developments, the reader is referred to the article by Andrew Gunder Frank, "Mexico: the Janus Faces of 20th-Century Bourgeois Revolution," which appeared in the November, 1962, issue of *MR*.) The secret of this political system, which in its essence is thoroughly totalitarian, is to retain in the hands of the ruling party (PRI) control over all mass organizations—the party itself, the national peasant federation, and the trade unions. Opposition parties have hardly had more than a token character, and attempts at genuinely independent action in either the political or the economic fields have been savagely repressed.

Under this setup, what was once a relatively large and powerful left-wing movement has been reduced in the course of the last two decades to a state of impotence. There are many revolutionaries in Mexico, among them some of the most famous intellectuals and artists in Latin America; but one can scarcely speak of a revolutionary movement at all. The Communist Party is very small and weak, and few people in Mexico take it seriously as a political force.

This doesn't mean that the status quo is permanently guaranteed in Mexico or that nothing of importance is happening there. On the contrary, the last two years have witnessed what may turn out to be the rebirth of a meaningful Left. The dominant figure in this new movement is Mexico's greatest living statesman, General Lázaro Cárdenas, under whose presidency in the 1930's the reforms introduced by the Revolution were consolidated and carried forward more than under any other President. In 1961, Cárdenas sponsored a Latin American Conference on National Sovereignty, Economic Emancipation, and Peace; and out of this conference there grew a new Mexican political organization, the Movement of National Liberation (MLN). This is not a political party, but it is laying the foundations on which a political party may be built in the future. This process of organizing outside the official apparatus was carried a step farther in early January of this year with the formation of a new Independent Peasant Central (CCI), with Cárdenas once again playing a leading role. The screams of anguish and vituperation which erupted from the bourgeois press at this development—the hysteria was at its peak while we were in Mexico City—are eloquent testimony that what may be called the "new Left" is beginning to make real headway. There is a tremendous amount of poverty, hunger, disease, and discontent in the Mexican countryside, and also in the "belts of misery" that girdle the rapidly growing urban centers. The ruling bourgeoisie knows it and fears nothing so much as the growth of independent and potentially revolutionary organizations to give voice to the voiceless and strength to the weak.

The next few years in Mexico will therefore probably be a critical period, with new struggles developing on various fronts and at various levels. But it is obvious that revolution is not now on the Mexican agenda.

## Chile

Chile presents an entirely different picture. Economically speaking, the country, like most of South America, is in a bad way, and the impossibility of achieving anything approaching a satisfactory rate of growth without far-reaching agrarian and other reforms is well understood. Furthermore, the Chilean political system is an entrenched form of parliamentary democracy in which political parties ranging from traditional conservative on the Right to Communist on the Left function freely and openly.* In addition, the Communist and Socialist Parties have a long record of working together and are now allied with each other and with a number of smaller parties and groups in a Popular Action Front (FRAP) which came very close to winning the last presidential election and is planning to run the same candidate, Salvador Allende, a popular and highly respected physician, in the next elections which are scheduled for the fall of 1964. Needless to say, hopes of an electoral victory are running high in the Chilean Left, and there is considerable confidence that democratic traditions are strong enough so that the FRAP, if elected, would be permitted to take office and put its program into effect. The program includes domestic reforms which stop far short of socialism and a foreign policy which can fairly be described as neutralist.

On the face of it, there is nothing revolutionary about either the methods or the objectives of the FRAP. Its domestic program, indeed, could almost be described as an implementation of the professed aims of the Alliance for Progress, and in this sense the Chilean Left is trying to impose on the bourgeoisie the reforms which it lacks the will to impose on itself. This does not mean, however, that the prospect of a FRAP victory is contemplated with equanimity by either the Chilean bourgeoisie or its American "Allies for Progress." On the contrary. The reforms now proposed are looked upon as merely a first installment, with more and worse to come later. And the FRAP's neutralist foreign policy is feared in Washington as the devil

---

* On successive days we had tea with Communist Deputies in the restaurant of the Chamber and with Socialist Senators in the restaurant of the Senate. The atmosphere and the attitudes of political opponents toward each other reminded us strongly of earlier visits to the House of Commons in London.

fears holy water. Let one country withdraw peacefully and quietly from the famous "inter-American system," so the reasoning goes, and the whole structure will come tumbling down. For these and other reasons, it seems clear to us that the ruling classes of Chile and the United States are going to fight the FRAP all the way down the line. Money will be poured out to win the elections for the bourgeois parties; and if this fails, a preventive coup d'état seems to us highly likely in spite of Chile's democratic traditions (in the peculiar logic of the bourgeoisie, military coups are sometimes necessary to *save* democracy—from the Communist menace of course: witness Guatemala).

Theoretically, a struggle of this kind might evoke a genuinely revolutionary response from the Chilean Left. It was, after all, the efforts of the U. S. and Cuban ruling classes to thwart and overthrow the Castro regime in Cuba that propelled that country further and further along the revolutionary road. And perhaps the same thing will happen in Chile. We hope so. But we would be less than candid if we failed to record our own strong impression that the Chilean Left, including the Communists, is not prepared, psychologically or in any other way, to meet the onslaught of reaction which it seems to us would inevitably follow a FRAP electoral victory. Under the circumstances, a successful revolutionary riposte seems rather unlikely. A FRAP government, taking office after a victory at the polls, could hardly be compared to the regime which was installed in power in Havana by the guns of a triumphant Rebel Army.

Chile provides what is perhaps the most striking example of a weakness which is common to most of the left-wing movements of Latin America (Venezuela is an exception which we shall discuss presently), namely, a lack of clarity about the nature of political power in class-riven, semi-colonial societies. The lesson of long historical experience is unambiguous: power, in Mao Tse-tung's famous phrase, grows out of the barrel of a gun. Neither the native ruling classes nor the imperialist overlords have any use for democratic forms except to the extent that they serve the needs of property and profits. Unless or until there is solid evidence to the contrary, responsible political leaders *must* assume that this state of affairs will continue to exist and must act accordingly. This does *not* mean they have to renounce peaceful and legal means of political struggle. What it means is that they must be prepared and must in every way prepare their followers for the renunciation of peaceful and legal means by the beneficiaries of the status quo. Electoral victories are important and may even be crucial; they should obviously be fought for whenever conditions make it possible. But it is essential to understand that they are the beginning, not the end, of the real struggle for power. It is this understanding which seems to us to be all too rare in the Latin American Left. More defeats and disappointments, we fear, will be suffered before the lesson is thoroughly learned.

### Argentina

Argentina is a big country, in many ways a rich country, a country with great potentialities. Buenos Aires, its capital, with more than six million inhabitants, broad tree-lined avenues, and numerous green parks and open spaces, reminds one of the great cities of Europe. The population is entirely of European extraction and has achieved a relatively high level of education and culture. And yet in spite of all these advantages, it is no exaggeration to say that Argentina today is in a state of economic and political disintegration. The economy is stagnant and unemployment is rising; at the very same time, the government operates with a whopping deficit and a perverse inflation runs its course. The regime in power is a thinly disguised military dictatorship which enjoys absolutely no popular support and even lacks the confidence of any important section of the bourgeoisie; it maintains a precarious state of law and order by arbitrary methods of repression but is unable to formulate, still less carry out, any positive policies to cope with the country's pressing problems. The traditional political parties, which got something like two-thirds of the votes in the last election (March, 1962), are at loggerheads and in any case have no programs worth taking seriously. The largest political group, the Peronists, which got the remaining third of the votes, is both illegal and at the same time being wooed by other groups and factions eager to use it for their own ends. However you look at it, the situation is a mess.

Well then, you may say, what Argentina needs is a revolution. There is no great mystery about what needs to be done.

135

Agriculture urgently needs to be strengthened; branches of the
economy producing for export need to be expanded and new
foreign markets opened; industrial development, which Argentina is quite capable of sustaining, needs to be planned in the
national interest; many new jobs need to be created and the
whole state apparatus needs to be reorganized and streamlined.
The present system, however, is totally incapable of tackling
these problems in a constructive way. What is needed therefore
is a new system, and that means revolution.

All this is undoubtedly true. But needing a revolution and
getting one are unfortunately two quite different things, and
Argentina's chances of getting one in the foreseeable future
seem to be very small indeed. The middle classes, which are
relatively numerous in Argentina, tend to be both conservative
and apathetic; while the active and militant section of the
working class is still under the spell of Peronism, which has no
clear ideology at all and only one solution to all problems: the
return of the great man. We are frank to admit that we mis-
understood and underestimated Peronism before we went to
Argentina. As a social phenomenon we still do not pretend to
understand it very well, but we no longer underestimate it. One
evening with a group of the most class-conscious and radical
Peronist trade union leaders convinced us of two things: that
the hold of Peronism on the Argentine proletariat is profound,
and that as long as this is the case the opportunities for growth
open to a genuine revolutionary movement will be very limited.

Under these conditions, it is of course not surprising that
the non-Peronist Left is small and divided. The old Socialist
Party, earliest of its kind in Latin America, has been split three
ways, and none of the resulting factions can be considered a
serious political force. The Communist Party is larger, but it too
is beset with internal divisions, and its traditional hostility to
Peronism has severely restricted its access to the proletarian
rank and file. It would be pleasant to be able to report, as in
the case of Mexico, signs of new organizational life on the
Argentine Left. Regretfully, we must say that we failed to de-
tect them. The number and quality of left-wing intellectuals and
artists seem to measure up to the standards of any other Latin
American country. The revolutionary movement, on the other
hand, is certainly one of the weakest in the whole region.

## Brazil

On the way from Argentina to Brazil we stopped over for a brief stay in Montevideo where we were received with customary Latin American hospitality and had an opportunity to become acquainted with representatives of all sections of the Uruguayan Left, including the editors of *Marcha*, one of the best political weeklies in the Western Hemisphere, which is much less known outside Uruguay than it deserves to be. If we nevertheless pass over Uruguay's problems, it is because the country is too small to play an independent role—it was created, as one Uruguayan friend put it, by the British to keep Brazil from sharing the Plata estuary with Argentina—and in the long run can only go the way its much larger and more powerful neighbors go.

Of these neighbors, Brazil, which has common frontiers with every South American country except Chile and Ecuador, is of course by far the largest both geographically and in terms of population. Moreover, Brazil has had the fastest rate of growth in recent years, and in the Rio-Sao Paulo-Belo Horizonte triangle possesses the most advanced industrial complex in Latin America. Brazilians are intensely nationalistic, proud of their achievements to date, and confident that within a matter of decades their country will become one of the leading powers in the world. In Argentina, one has the feeling of having come to a dead end with no way out in sight. In Brazil, on the contrary, one has the feeling of traveling fast through open country even if one is not very sure what the road is like ahead.

In these circumstances, the Brazilian political agenda is concerned with reform, not with revolution. Once again, as in the case of Argentina, there is no mystery about what is needed: agriculture must be modernized if the rapidly increasing urban population is to be fed, the urgent need for more exports is to be met, and a growing internal market is to be created; the balance of payments must be brought under control and foreign debts consolidated and reduced; the wild inflation of recent years—fruit of huge government deficits which in turn stem from lavish politically-motivated subsidies and a tax system which lets the rich off lightly—must be curbed; the impoverished and potentially explosive Northeast must be brought into the process of economic development; and to accomplish these and related goals the present helter-skelter growth of industry must be shaped and directed in accordance with a rational plan. The sixty-four dollar question in Brazil is whether the bourgeoisie can make these necessary reforms, or at least enough of them to enable a reasonably high rate of growth to be maintained.

For reasons which were summarized above, we do not think the chances are very good. The kind of agrarian reform and development that Brazil will need as its population shoots up in the years ahead (the rate of growth is one of the highest in the world) is much more radical than anything the Brazilian bourgeoisie has yet begun to think about. We do not believe it will rise to the task, especially since doing so would be bound to impose sacrifices on some of its own influential sectors. Nor do we believe that the Brazilian bourgeoisie will be willing to fight for the degree of independence from the U. S. which would be a necessary condition for establishing control over the country's balance of payments and introducing a reasonably effective system of overall planning. These are judgments which we are quite frank to admit are based largely on general inferences from past experience—that is to say, on theory—and which closer acquaintance with specific Brazilian conditions might lead us to modify. Further study is called for, but time alone of course will give the final answers.

In the meantime, what does the Brazilian Left think about these matters and what course of action is it charting? There is of course no single answer to this question, but all the same it seemed to us that there was a fairly broad consensus among leftists we talked to, including both Communists and independents. (There is no significant Socialist Party in Brazil, and the party which calls itself Social Democratic is one of the large conservative parties.) In the first place, the Left has no confidence whatever in the present Goulart government which it regards as fairly representative of the Brazilian bourgeoisie. Nor does it believe that the bourgeoisie, left to its own devices, will introduce and carry through the necessary reforms. It does not conclude from this, however, that Brazil must sooner or later take the revolutionary path and that it is therefore necessary to begin to develop a movement with revolution as its aim. Instead, it believes that the Left can develop enough political

138

SWEEZY AND HUBERMAN

weight to force the bourgeoisie to accept what is sometimes referred to as a "popular government" which, with the backing of the masses, will put through the needed reforms. Presumably, this will be accomplished through a combination of electoral politics and mass pressure. Making allowances for national variations, this seems to us to be essentially the same perspective held by the Chilean Left, the main difference being that the Chileans expect to achieve success in the near future while even the most optimistic Brazilians see a long pull ahead.

There is another version of this theory which seems to be gaining adherents among younger functionaries in the state apparatus, especially those in the various public enterprises which play an important role in the Brazilian economy. This is that the trained economists and technocrats who manage these enterprises and man the government departments and agencies that deal with economic matters can become representatives of an objectively demonstrable national interest which, when the people become sufficiently aware of it, no government will dare to contravene. In either version, the state is assumed to play a relatively independent economic role and to follow the dictates not of ruling-class interests but rather of the interests of the nation as a whole.

Theories of this kind (and one meets them in many versions in many lands) are of course nothing really new, nor do we believe they are any more valid in Brazil than they have turned out to be elsewhere. The Brazilian Left, like its Chilean counterpart, will learn this sooner or later, but it may take longer in Brazil than in Chile.

## Venezuela

Before we got to Venezuela, we heard stories about the crazy leftists in that country who were trying to stage insurrections without any real hope of success and thus were dissipating their forces and depriving the country of a meaningful opposition to the Betancourt government.

We found the reality to be very different. The two largest organizations of the Venezuelan Left are the Communist Party and the Left Revolutionary Movement (MIR) which broke off several years ago from Betancourt's ruling Democratic Action Party; and we were fortunate to be able to meet and discuss at

NOTES ON LATIN AMERICA

length with leaders and members of both groups. They are
wonderful people who are carrying on a gallant struggle under
very difficult conditions. They are in no sense irresponsible ad-
venturists; and, as Dr. Betancourt knows better than anyone
else, they are maintaining an opposition which is more meaningful and effective than that faced by any other regime in Latin
America today.

Tactically, the Venezuelan Left is both skilled and flexible.
They use every legal method open to them, but when they meet
with repression, which is very often, they fight back in kind.
Pitched battles have been fought against Betancourt's police
(everywhere in evidence and all carrying machine guns), and
a substantial guerrilla campaign is being waged in the mountains of the state of Falcon, in the northwestern part of the
country. No one knows how many guerrillas are now active,
and the government blows hot and cold on the subject. But the
latest official figure, issued a couple of months ago, was 3,000
which, if anywhere near the truth, is a very impressive figure
indeed, many more than Fidel Castro ever had with him in
the Sierra Maestra. The purpose of the armed struggle, as of
the struggle by non-violent means, is not, as many seem to think,
to overthrow the government and seize power. The leaders know
perfectly well that under present conditions, international as
well as national, this is not a feasible goal. The purpose is to
force the government to change its policies, to drop its repressive methods, to move vigorously to secure a larger share of oil
revenues for Venezuela, and to use these revenues in a planned
way for the benefit of the masses. The Left is under no illusions
that these aims can be fully achieved without a socialist revolution, but it thinks the only effective way to achieve any part
of them is through militant struggle, and, no less important, that
only through militant struggle can the masses be politically and
psychologically prepared to make the revolution when the time
is ripe.

The widespread support which the Left enjoys is proved
by the fact that the very heart of the movement is in the Central
University in Caracas which has some of the aspects of a revolutionary enclave in hostile territory. To go to the University,
to talk to dozens of students from many schools and departments, to be privileged to address a large audience (even after

a move from a smaller to a larger auditorium, some 500 persons had to be turned away for lack of space)—these were the most thrilling experiences of our Latin American trip. Nor is left-wing and revolutionary sentiment confined to students: it is also widespread in the faculties of the University. Among economists, for example, we would hazard the guess that there are proportionately as many revolutionaries in the School of Economics at the University of Caracas as there are (or were) New Frontiersmen at Harvard or unreconstructed champions of laissez faire at Chicago.

It is this massive support enjoyed by the Left at the University that has prevented Betancourt from taking over the institution and extinguishing its traditional autonomy. After all, he knows that his own political career began at the University where he and his fellow student conspirators plotted the overthrow of the Gomez dictatorship. And he must know in his heart of hearts that the true aspirations of the nation are still expressed by the gallant revolutionaries at the very center of the nation's intellectual life.

No, the leftists of Venezuela are not crazy, far from it. They, along with Fidel Castro and the generation of Cubans who are for the first time bringing socialism to the Americas, are the salt of the earth. For whatever mistakes they may make, history will absolve them. And for keeping the revolutionary banner high despite all difficulties and dangers, history will honor them.

## Latin American Students

Lacking space to attempt a fuller analysis of the political situation in the countries visited, we must be content to conclude these notes with a few general comments on topics of current interest.

Not only in Venezuela but in every country, we were very favorably impressed by the students we met. To be sure, there are plenty of things wrong with the kind of education they are getting. The secondary schools and universities are still largely oriented toward the education of a small elite. Teachers are often poorly qualified and badly paid, with the result that they spend most of their time on other jobs and neglect their teaching duties. Living arrangements are unsatisfactory and facilities such as libraries and laboratories are sadly inadequate. All this and much more is undoubtedly true, but these are not the things that are likely to make the deepest impression on a visitor from the United States. In this country, student life is something apart from the life of the larger society. By and large, students feel that their whole responsibility is to themselves: they must get the right ideas, make the right connections, and acquire the right training so that when they get through with their formal education they can marry the right mate, get the right job, and bring up children who will in due course be ready to repeat the cycle. From infancy up, they are taught that if you take care of yourself you are doing your social duty; the other side of the coin is that if you fail to take care of yourself you are no good and deserve whatever comes to you. Whether anyone really believes these classic tenets of bourgeois thought any longer is an open question. Probably very few do, which makes the whole situation much worse. Nobody really believes anything. Life becomes directed to survival, having a "good time," and avoiding unpleasantness. Nothing else really matters.*

Students in Latin America are different. They have ideals. They think first of their country, not of themselves. The idea of living and sacrificing for something larger and nobler than their own private interests comes naturally to them. They *care*. And that makes all the difference.

Of course, many of them will be corrupted by the vile social reality into which they must graduate. The cynical "realist" who was a revolutionary in his youth is a familiar figure in Latin America. In fact, the governments of the region are full of them. They are the best "friends" of the United States.

But not all students travel that path, and we are convinced that the number who do not will increase from year to year. They are learning, more from history than from formal studies, that the ideals of their youth—patriotism, a better life for all, human dignity and solidarity—are not necessarily illusions but can become the realistic goals of meaningful lives. And in increasing numbers they are accepting the fact that this means

---

* This description does not fit Negro students in the South struggling against the iniquities of segregation. But they are, of course, a small minority of the total U.S. student body.

revolutionary activity with all its dangers and rewards. It is from the ranks of these students that the future Latin American Fidel Castros and Che Guevaras will emerge.

Meanwhile, we would like to recommend to any U. S. students who may have the opportunity that they go to one of the larger Latin American universities for a year or more of study. In some respects, you may not learn as much as you would at home. But you'll learn a lot more about the world you live in. And you may even learn to live.

## Attitudes Toward Cuba

We did not meet a single serious leftist in Latin America who is not an ardent supporter of the Cuban Revolution. They understand perfectly the motivation and aims of U. S. policy toward Cuba. The bogey of Communism doesn't scare them, and the more the U. S. builds it up the less they fear it. They know what has been accomplished in Cuba and accept the setbacks and hardships that have had to be endured as unavoidable and for the most part the work of the imperialists. There is just one thing that worries them, the extent to which Cuba, in resisting the U. S., may have fallen under the domination of the Soviet Union. The desire for national independence is a real passion in Latin America, and any encroachment on the sovereignty of any brother country is looked upon with abhorrence.

Against this background, it is easy to understand that the October crisis caused great concern among Latin American leftists. Few of them have ever given any thought to the strategic policies of the atomic powers—there do not even seem to be accepted translations of such terms as "first strike," "counterforce," "minimum deterrent," and so on—and many were either confused by the sudden appearance of Soviet missile sites in Cuba or believed the official U. S. explanation that they were put there for offensive purposes. Since it obviously could not be to the interest of Cuba to become a base for offensive action against the U. S., this planted the idea, or at least the suspicion, that Cuba was being used. And when Khrushchev made the agreement to pull the missiles out without consulting Fidel, the fears and doubts were intensified.

If the initial impact of the crisis was altogether negative, subsequent developments have done much to repair the damage. Fidel's rejection of unilateral inspection was not the act of a puppet, and Latins are very sensitive to things of this sort—much more so than the people of the U. S. The Cuban demand for an agreement with the U. S. on the basis of the Five Points has full backing, and Soviet support for the Five Points made a good impression. Moreover, we found that the people to whom we talked were very receptive to our argument (developed in the December Review of the Month) that the Soviet placement of missiles, whether or not it was a wise move, could not possibly have had any strategic aim other than to deter an attack on Cuba. In time, we believe, the Latin American Left will come around to the realization that in the present international situation, both as between East and West and within the socialist bloc itself, Cuba's position is a good deal stronger than it at first sight appears to be. Militarily, Cuba cannot be anything but a danger and a liability to the USSR. If nevertheless, the Soviet leaders find good reasons for continuing to extend protection to the little island, this can only mean that it is Cuba that is using the Soviet Union rather than the other way around.

### Socialism and Economic Development

One final point. One frequently meets the argument that Latin America (as well as other underdeveloped areas of the world) must have socialism because capitalism, which is inseparable from imperialism, is incapable of generating the kind and degree of economic development that is absolutely essential to provide rising living standards for rapidly growing populations. We believe that this is so, but we think it is a great mistake for socialists to rest their case there.

Take a good, long look at the kind of societies that have been emerging in such relatively progressive Latin American countries as Mexico and Brazil. Then suppose, which is not the case, that there were no barriers to their growing faster and indefinitely. Would there then be no case for socialism in these countries? Is sheer quantitative economic development as such all that is important?

We think not. Mexico and Brazil are in fact horrible examples of what happens to an underdeveloped country that encourages a process of industrialization based on the private automobile. You can get a lot of factories that way, and no doubt the people who work in the factories are better off than they used to be. But you also get a lot of automobiles and the kind of congested, polluted, stinking cities that go with the automobiles. These cities in turn act as magnets for the half-starving people of the countryside who flock into the Hoovertowns that surround them—"callampas" in Santiago, "favelas" in Rio, "ranchos" in Caracas: every country has its name for them. These people too may be better off than they were; otherwise they wouldn't continue to crowd into the cities. But they don't own automobiles and never expect to, and most of them will never get jobs producing automobiles either. The industrialization of the country neither gives them employment nor serves their needs. God knows how they manage to live, but there is little evidence that He cares. (Passing them by every day and seeing them in their misery tends to make everyone else callous to their fate as well.) It is of course worse in the countryside: capitalism's way of "solving" the problem of agriculture—if indeed it has any solution—is to ruin most farmers while enriching a few.

It simply won't do, and socialists should never stop saying so. Capitalism must be rejected not only, and not even primarily, because it fails to generate sufficiently rapid development. It must be rejected above all because it fails to provide a society and an environment worthy of human beings.

(February 18, 1963)